The Infinite
Desire for Growth

The Infinite Desire for Growth

Daniel Cohen

Translated by Jane Marie Todd

PRINCETON UNIVERSITY PRESS

Princeton & Oxford

This book was originally published as *Le monde est clos et le desir infini* by Albin Michel, Paris, France, and is copyright © Éditions Albin Michel— Paris 2015. This English translation is copyright © 2018 by Princeton University Press

Published by Princeton University Press, 41 William Street, Princeton, New Jersey 08540

In the United Kingdom: Princeton University Press, 6 Oxford Street, Woodstock, Oxfordshire OX20 1TR

press.princeton.edu

ISBN 978-0-691-17253-8

Library of Congress Control Number: 2017958886

British Library Cataloging-in-Publication Data is available

Editorial: Sarah Caro and Hannah Paul
Production Editorial: Debbie Tegarden
Text Design: Leslie Flis
Jacket illustration and design by Faceout Studio, Derek Thornton
Production: Erin Suydam
Publicity: Andrew DeSio and Caroline Priday
Copyeditor: Elizabeth Stone

The translation of this book has been aided by Centre National du Livre

This book has been composed in Sabon LT Std

Printed on acid-free paper. ∞

Printed in the United States of America

1 3 5 7 9 10 8 6 4 2

For Pauline, my baby,
who also had to read this book

The ignorance of its material conditions
leads mankind to err dangerously.

Georges Bataille, *La Part maudite*

Contents

∾

Acknowledgments

The author wishes to thank Sarah Caro, the editor of the English version of the book, for her wonderful work. Her thoughtful reading and re-reading of the manuscript has made this edition a much better piece than the French original. Many thanks too to Jane Marie Todd for her superb translation.

The Infinite
Desire for Growth

∾

Introduction

Economic growth is the religion of the modern world, the elixir that eases the pain of social conflicts, the promise of indefinite progress. It offers a solution to the everyday drama of human life, to wanting what we don't have. Sadly, at least in the West, growth is now fleeting, intermittent. It comes and goes, with bust following boom and boom following bust, while an ideal world of steady, inclusive, long-lasting growth fades away.

Historians have spoken of a crisis of the "European conscience" to characterize the profound spiritual angst that struck Europe in the seventeenth century, when, through Galileo and Johannes Kepler, it discovered that the universe is empty, that the stars are not the dwelling place of the gods. Is life worth living, our ancestors asked, deprived of the divine promise of salvation? We are experiencing a crisis of the same nature. The very idea of progress seems to be negated when growth disappears. Today the question has become: Will our lives be harsh and sad if the promise of material progress is taken away from us?

The great English economist John Maynard Keynes, writing at the outset of the economic crisis of the 1930s, warned against the pessimism of his time, and his message remains refreshingly hopeful. Despite the crisis looming all around, he wrote in his famous article "Economic Possibilities for Our Grandchildren" that a period of exceptional prosperity was at hand and that the world's "economic problem" would soon be resolved—just as, in the preceding century, the problem of providing enough food had been solved. Based on existing patterns of industrial growth he boldly announced that by 2030 people would work three hours a day and be able to devote themselves to the really important tasks of art, culture, and metaphysics. Sadly, questions of culture and metaphysics have not become the defining issues of our day. The pursuit of material wealth remains our primary goal, despite the fact that we in the West are four times richer than we were in the 1930s. Thus it must be said that while Keynes, an intellectual giant, perfectly predicted the prosperity to come, he failed completely to foresee what we would make of it. Like many before him, he did not understand the extraordinary malleability of human desire, which is prepared to consume boundless riches to find its place in the world.

The so-called Easterlin paradox helps to explain Keynes's mistake. According to the economist Richard Easterlin, wealth does not correlate well with happiness. A higher salary is obviously always desirable, yet once we've reached that target it is never enough. We fall victim to a process of habituation of which we are largely unaware. Furthermore, as each of us sets our own goals, we fail to take into account how much our desires depend upon the achievements of the others. If they get richer, we also want more riches for ourselves. "Once the basic needs are satisfied, and sometimes even before," writes the philosopher René Girard, "humans feel intense desire, but they do not know for what. For it is being they desire, a 'beingness' of which they feel deprived and which, it seems to them, others have." This explains why economic growth, more than pure wealth, is the key to the functioning of our society: for it provides each of us with the hope that we can rise above our present condition, even though this dream remains elusive.

The idea of progress has been subject to serious misunderstandings throughout history. The Enlightenment, which introduced the idea in the eighteenth century, made progress a moral value, one of autonomy and freedom, using it to critique the hierarchical order of the *Ancien Régime*. The Industrial Revolution, which unfolded in Europe over the course of the nineteenth century, transformed that ideal into a promise of material progress. Yet in doing so, it also established a society that completely turned its back on Enlightenment ideals. Engineers drove out priests, but industrial society remained just as hierarchical as before. In the family and in the factory, the vertical structure of society continued to dominate. In the twentieth century, Fordism and the assembly line, the standard for the industrial world, retained the age-old pyramidal organizational structure. In the private sphere, it was not until 1965 that a woman in France could open a bank account without her husband's permission. Some two centuries after the French Revolution, she was still under his guardianship when it came to most of the legal acts that affected her. For women, as for many other social groups, the idea of autonomy and freedom was dead on arrival.

It is only in the last few decades that the remaining vestiges of the *Ancien Régime* have finally disappeared. Workers no longer manipulate physical objects (agricultural or industrial), but rather the flow of information. According to the sociologist Ronald Inglehart, creativity is replacing authority as the core value. In his view, Enlightenment ideas are finally prevailing: autonomy and self-direction are becoming the standard of our modernity. Sadly, it is not so simple. The new digital economy is setting in place a totally disruptive "zero-cost" production model, bringing in new forms of insecurity. Inexpensive software takes over routine tasks, whatever their level of sophistication, from playing chess to dispensing cash to trading on the stock market. This race against machines creates a nervous strain that is reaching new heights. As the economists David Blanchflower and Andrew Oswald have shown, mental stress in the workplace has increased over the years. To borrow an expression from the psychoanalyst Pierre Legendre, modern man lives above his "psychological means." Creativity, when it becomes a business imperative, loses much of its moral benefit.

Inglehart, furthermore, repeats Keynes's error when he concludes that a postmaterialist world, freed from need, is now at hand. The quest for economic growth is still very much there, for the reasons explained by the Easterlin paradox. But digital society is marked by a paradox of its own: the technological prospects it heralds have never looked so bright, yet the prospects for growth have never been so disappointing. We seem to be experiencing *an industrial revolution without growth*. In the United States, 90 percent of the population has seen no growth in purchasing power over the last thirty years. In France, annual per capita growth has dropped steadily from 3 percent in the 1970s to 2 and then 1 percent in the following decades, and down to almost zero in the last five years. This brings us back to the critical question: Will economic growth for the broader population return, and if it doesn't, what then?

Economists are sharply divided. The pessimists, led by Robert Gordon, believe that the potential for economic growth is now much lower than in the last century. In his book *The Rise and Fall of American Growth*, he explains that the new industrial revolution may have given us the smartphone, but that hardly compares, in his thinking, to the great advances of the twentieth century: electricity, the automobile, the airplane, movies, television, antibiotics. On the other hand, optimists like Erik Brynjolfsson and Andrew McAfee tell us in their book *The Second Machine*

Age that Moore's Law is going to allow "the digitization of just about everything." Already, we have driverless cars, and robots are caring for the elderly in Japan: Another burst of growth appears to be at hand.

When analyzing this controversy in detail, it becomes apparent that this is less a clash between those who believe in technology and those who don't than an argument about whether the new pattern of growth is inclusive or not. Are the new technologies dragging workers in or out of the vanguard of economic growth? It's useful to compare this situation with the twentieth century when American farmers, comprising 40 percent of the labor force in 1900, moved to the cities and became highly productive workers in manufacturing. Economic growth quickly doubled. The fact that the purchasing power of the American middle class has grown so little over the last thirty years reflects a major change: Workers have been let go from the most efficient factories—but their productivity in their new jobs is often stagnant, which explains why economic growth is petering out (something economists refer to as the Baumol disease).

So how could we deal with a world without the kind of economic growth that we experienced in the previous century—if that were to come to pass? How do we motivate people if we can't fulfill their hopes for rising living standards? One recalls the radical move by Henry Ford to double salaries in his factories to cut back on absenteeism and to reinvigorate his employees' desire to work. In growing economies you can reward diligent workers with rising wages. Today's companies do give bonuses to workers based on merit, but that carrot comes with a stick: layoffs if goals aren't met.

Work hard or get laid off, as opposed to work hard and get higher wages: this management-by-stress technique is a major cause of suffering in our modern societies, and it is simply counterproductive. Unhappy workers are less productive, less cooperative, and less creative. Can't we do better? The Danish economic model, much discussed in Europe, shows that it is indeed possible to motivate workers by something other than fear. Denmark's ample safety net protecting laid-off workers and providing job retraining encourages mobility in the workplace and eases fears about losing one's job. The country ranks highest in job quality in Europe. It's no wonder then that in 2013 Denmark was declared the happiest country in the world.

It would be absurd to argue that the ills of Western societies all arise from the stagnation of individual purchasing power. But if we ignore the problem and go on pretending that growth will surely return, just as it did after World War II, we will fail to understand the reasons why weak economic growth produces an unhappy society. We must try to imagine a world in which happiness and satisfaction with one's life are less dependent on the expectation of constantly earning more. This will take us on a long journey to understand how human desires have been fulfilled throughout history, what has been the role of modern economic growth in the quest for happiness, and how we might reinvent the idea of progress beyond material gains.

PART I

The Origin of Growth

CHAPTER 1

The Human Species

Is economic growth intrinsic to mankind? It sounds like a crazy question: growth is usually portrayed as a relatively new phenomenon, dating back only two centuries. From the mists of time until the Industrial Revolution in the eighteenth century, human beings' income stagnated at a level close to that of the poorest people now living, about a dollar a day. Growth, in the sense of a continuous rise in per capita income, is the major innovation of the modern world. If, however, we allow for a more flexible time frame, counting technological and organizational progress in millennia, rather than in centuries, or as we do now in decades, growth, both of populations and in the number of innovations they produce, does go back much further in history. One may indeed venture to say that it is part of human history.

Two Big Bangs altered the course of our existence within an extremely brief time frame, when measured against the history of the human species. The first was the invention of agriculture, which caused a population explosion that continues even today. The human population grew from 5 million ten thousand years ago to 200 million in the time of Christ, and might reach 10 billion by 2050, at which date it could stabilize. Agriculture gave birth to writing, money, metallurgy, the printing press, the compass, and gunpowder.

The second Big Bang was the scientific revolution of the seventeenth century, which gave new impetus to human knowledge, and its growth too was exponential. To take just one recent example among many thousand: according to an original estimate by the economist William Nordhaus, the cost of making a standardized set of calculations has dropped by a factor of more than a billion in the last fifty years.

We are now witnessing the dawn of a third Big Bang, when these two forces are beginning to resonate, each gaining strength from the other. Paul Crutzen, winner of the Nobel prize in chemistry, characterizes our epoch as the "Anthropocene," which marks a transition from a world dominated by nature to one dominated by human beings. One statistic in and of itself sums up the significance of that term. During the era when agriculture developed, human beings, their herds, and other domestic animals represented less than 0.1 percent of all mammals on earth. They now represent more than 90 percent.

Faced with the extraordinary challenge of living in a finite world overrun by their presence, human beings have to start thinking collectively about the consequences of their actions. Up until now, we have not made the effort, swept up in a historical evolution whose real significance we have generally understood only in hindsight. To regain control of our future, we must retrace that history. How and why did economic growth, in the sense we currently understand that expression, first appear? What particular causes explain why it originally emerged in the West rather than in China or elsewhere? Should that be seen as the sign of a lasting philosophical, political, and moral superiority or as a phase that has already passed? These are decisive questions for understanding the origins of our addiction to growth and how to handle it.

HOMO SAPIENS

The first hominids appeared six to eight million years ago, and nothing would have allowed one to predict that they would one day rule the planet. Ants and termites took about a hundred million years to gain possession of the world below ground, giving other species the time to adapt. Humans have occupied the earth much more quickly, and, in a quite extraordinary fashion, now seem bent on destroying it.

The most ancient fossils date back seven million years: they are those of Toumai, a member of the species *Sahelanthropus tchadensis*, whose brain capacity was that of a present-day chimpanzee. Then came *Australopithecus afarensis*, the "Lucy" species (Lucy was discovered by Yves Coppens in 1974, and her name is an *homage* to a Beatles song). Then, a subgroup differentiated itself: *Homo habilis*, which appeared two and a half million years ago and vanished seven hundred thousand years later. Because the climate was becoming dryer, the savannah replaced the forests where *Homo habilis* was living (the long arms characteristic of members of this group suggest they were often in the trees). *Homo erectus* (in tandem with a cousin, *Homo ergaster*) came next, marking the beginning of a tremendous change in the brain. The philosopher Francis Wolff seems amused by our abundance of ancestors: "Even recently, we were looking for a common ancestor of human beings and apes, but that question is gradually losing its pertinence. What about Flores man or the mysterious Denisovans, and what about all the fossil human species that will unfailingly be discovered in the future, which will be new blows to 'our' humanity?"[1] In any

---

[1] "La question de l'homme aujourd'hui," *Le Débat* (May–August 2014).

case, abstract thought, syntactical language, long-term memory, and the ability to construct hypothetical scenarios, to cooperate within the group, and to predict the intentions of one's enemies now constituted the formidable tool kit of the human brain.[2]

According to Michael Tomasello, a specialist in evolutionary anthropology, humans' superiority lies in their power to collaborate with others to achieve common goals. As Edward O. Wilson puts it, "We have become the experts at mind reading, and the world champions at inventing culture."[3] Hunter-gatherers and Wall Street traders gossip at every opportunity. The sociable nature of human beings bears a superficial resemblance to that of insects, which are also capable of a remarkable division of labor in service of the reproduction of the species. But cooperation amongst bees is not really "cooperative" in origin: the queen alone controls the reproduction of her genetic inheritance. She travels great distances and severs her ties with her original colony to constitute her own. The human species has more subtle and flexible resources at its disposal: a combination of altruism, domination, reciprocity, betrayal, and deceit allows human beings to play out their destiny on the great stage of social life.

Most of the ideas that occur to animals die with them. Female chimpanzees teach their young to crack nuts and to strip the leaves off plant stems to catch termites, but human language, which far surpasses the language of

---

[2] *Homo habilis* was the first hominid with a brain whose volume surpassed 1,000 cm^3, compared to 360 for Toumai and 1,350 for us.

[3] Edward O. Wilson, *The Social Conquest of Earth* (New York: Liveright, 2012), p. 226; see also Michael Tomasello, *The Cultural Origins of Human Cognition* (Cambridge, Mass.: Harvard University Press, 1999).

other animals in its complexity, allows us to learn collectively. We share 98.4 percent of our DNA with chimpanzees. As individuals, we are not a great deal brighter than our simian cousins. As a species, however, we fare much better. The human brain should not be compared to that of chimpanzees. Rather, it is the combined total of all human intelligence that must be measured against that of all chimpanzees.

Throughout its history, humanity has invented techniques for accumulating and diffusing knowledge that vastly increased its technical and social power. Writing, currency, and then, much later, the printing press, the telephone, and the Internet are all technologies that have allowed us to create a collective intelligence with no equivalent among the other animal species.

The brain combines a capacity to be highly intelligent, even computerlike, with the emotionality of a love-struck adolescent. Both selfish and altruistic, rational and emotional—how did our species reconcile these contradictory qualities? According to Wilson's research, presented in *The Social Conquest of Earth*, two biological traits lie behind these propensities: our (large) size and (limited) mobility. Granted, humans are small compared to dinosaurs, but we are very big relative to insects, which are not of a size to control fire or sizeable objects. Insects on the other hand travel far and quickly, thus avoiding contact with other groups. Humans, with their low degree of mobility, must live with their fellows, whether in peace or in conflict. Although incapable of running as fast as their prey—antelopes, zebras, or ostriches—they can track them over long distances. They also learned to use projectiles (stones, and later spears or arrows) to hunt animals, as well as fire to cook the meat.

THE INVENTION OF CULTURE

Tribal membership and the defense of the tribe against rival groups are among the fundamental traits of human nature. Theories such as that of the selfish gene are appealing because they seem to explain the astonishing concomitance in many species, not just mankind, of altruism and individualism. A typical example of this is the male praying mantis, which allows itself to be devoured by the female to ensure the reproduction of the species. But the underpinnings of human tribalism are much more complex than the mechanical reproduction of genes. Psychology experiments conducted on college students have shown how quickly, and altogether arbitrarily, groups form among human beings. If one subgroup of strangers who share no genetic heritage is given red cards and another blue cards, solidarity forms among those given the same colors. And boundaries between various groups are totally malleable: families, alliances, and guilds all give individuals a home, or more than one home, within a chaotic world.

In *The Elementary Structures of Kinship*, Claude Lévi-Strauss explains that the human species is the only one to have domesticated itself. In his view, the prohibition of incest was the founding moment when culture prevailed over nature: if I give my daughter in exchange for yours, our clans will live in peace. The capacity to create prohibitions and classifications without any basis in biology is one of the recurrent traits of human beings. According to Lévi-Strauss, in some societies a girl may (sometimes must) marry the son of her maternal uncle but not the son of her paternal uncle, even though, from a genetic standpoint, there is no difference between the two cases. The difference is entirely cultural. Such is the foundation of culture: it sets down rules, however arbitrary from a genetic perspective, that establish the modalities of social life.

Culture is not the monopoly of humankind, however, when defined as a set of rules that organize the life of a group. Female chimpanzees will join adjacent communities, whereas the gregarious males must secure their position within their original group. African wolves and wild dogs have an elaborate social organization, whereby hunters bring food back to the alpha female and the newborns. Chimpanzees and bonobos hunt in packs. Bonobos engage in exuberant, nonreproductive sexual activity, which serves to relieve the stress of a very emotional species. Empathy can also be found among the rhesus macaques. And the violence of young chimpanzee "gangs" against their peers is remarkably similar to that of their human counterparts.

In all species, survival requires the group's cooperation to confront predators. Conversely, within the group, male competition for females favors the tenet "every one for himself." These two traits are not always mutually compatible: nature does not necessarily do things well every time. One gazelle must run faster than the others to escape its predators and, ultimately, that is a good thing for the species as a whole. By contrast, as Darwin noted in his analysis of peacocks, the magnificent colored plumage of the males allows them to seduce females but is also a hindrance when fleeing predators. Stags have antlers that allow them to vanquish their rivals, but at the cost of reduced mobility, which is a handicap. It is logical for males to want to attract females on an individual basis, but that sometimes occurs to the detriment of the species.[4]

[4] Robert Frank, *The Darwin Economy* (Princeton, N.J.: Princeton University Press, 2011).

WHAT IS HUMANKIND?

Let us turn, then, to the key question, "What distinguishes humans from the other species?" Freud put it this way: "Why do our relatives, the animals, not exhibit any such cultural struggle?"[5] By "such cultural struggle," he means discontent, anxiety, the torment of existence. Alone among animals, writes Pierre Legendre, human beings "ask questions about their presence, the very fact of their own existence."[6] In *Oedipus at Colonus*, Sophocles says it would be better not to be born. All cultures are propelled by the human question par excellence: Who am I, and what is the purpose of life?

The simplest way to characterize a human being is to say it is a speaking animal, in search of someone who will listen and respond and acknowledge them. As Pierre Legendre also says, the "revolutionary" fact of the human species is the demand for legitimacy. Betrayal is never easy for us, even when the circumstances call for it. A permanent tension exists within us between honor, virtue, duty, and their opposites: selfishness, cowardice, hypocrisy. Culture, including art, expresses this conflict, a constant throughout human history, and also contributes toward its resolution.

"We are the only species that not only lives in society, like the other animal species, but that produces new forms of social existence, and hence of culture, in order to go on living. To always be creating, not simply recreating, society is what is unique about human beings." That is the answer proposed by Maurice Godelier in the

---

[5]Sigmund Freud, *Civilization and Its Discontents*, trans. James Strachey (New York: W. W. Norton, 1961), chap. 7, p. 70.

[6]Pierre Legendre, *Ce que l'Occident ne voit pas de l'Occident: Conférences au Japon* (Paris: Mille et une nuits, 2004).

conclusion to a book on Lévi-Strauss.[7] The social games of animals do not evolve, or do so very little. There are no soccer games, no violent videos or online pornography for young apes. Over the course of civilizations, we humans play at modifying the rules. We changed the model of kinship, the fertility rate, and can (sometimes) contain the violence within us. The critical problem identified by the French philosopher Georges Bataille,[8] however, is that each civilization has a tendency to take as inviolable the rules that it has created and prefers to go along with them, right up to the point of exhaustion, rather than change them, when needed.

[7] Maurice Godelier, *Lévi-Strauss* (Paris: Seuil, 2013).
[8] Georges Bataille, *La part maudite* (Paris: Minuit, 1949; reissued 2014).

CHAPTER 2

Exodus

About a hundred thousand years ago, a period of extreme aridity struck tropical Africa.[1] At the time, humanity in its nascent state came very close to extinction. Its numbers dropped to a few (tens of) thousands. Then the great drought ended. The tropical forests and the savannah gradually recovered their luxuriance. Better climate conditions allowed for an increase in the number of people, who forged a path to the Nile and the Sinai. After passing through the Nile Valley, then the Levant, *Homo sapiens* entered Europe in about 40,000 B.C.E., occupying the territory that had already been inhabited by a similar species, Neanderthal, for some two hundred thousand years.[2]

Shortly after the arrival of *Homo sapiens*, the Neanderthals disappeared, no doubt because of the imprint the newcomer left on their ecosystem.[3] The Neanderthals practiced "big-game" hunting, took care of their injured, and buried their dead. One hypothesis about the differences between them and *Homo sapiens* is that the

[1]Earth's solar orbit is not perfectly circular because of the gravitational pull of the other planets. That accounts for the ice ages: there have been between forty and fifty since the planet came into being, including one 190,000 and another 50,000 years ago.

[2]Fifty to sixty thousand years ago, before *Homo sapiens* reached Europe, other migrations, to India and Southeast Asia, had taken place.

[3]In southern Siberia, *Homo sapiens* undoubtedly contributed to the extinction of a nearby species, the Denisovans, to whom Francis Wolff has given his attention.

Neanderthals may have had less of an ability to speak, perhaps because of a poor placement of the larynx[4]—despite possessing the FOXP2 gene, responsible for language.

THE INVENTION OF AGRICULTURE

Then came the great upheaval: the invention of agriculture about ten thousand years ago (and subsequently, in eight different places), which would turn the relationship between humans and nature on its head. Modifications in the climate once again played a role. A warming of the climate (in about 9600 B.C.E.) may have been the cause. Three hundred years later, barley and wheat were being cultivated in the Jordan Valley, and grains significantly larger than the wild versions were being consumed. In "less than a thousand years," as Ian Morris, a professor at Stanford University, put it, agriculture became a science. Lentil and chickpea dishes made their appearance.[5] Human beings learned to sew clothing. And animals were put to more efficient use. They were no longer killed immediately for their meat, but were raised for their wool and milk, or to pull carts.

That invention set off a population explosion that is still under way. It quashed biodiversity, because the other species had no way to adapt to our evolution in such a short time. Between 10,000 and 7000 B.C.E., the use and manufacture of stone tools increased, and farmers

---

[4]Neanderthals were hugely carnivorous. They possessed brains larger than our own (1,520 cm³, compared to 1,350). *Homo sapiens* shares between one and four percent of its genes with Neanderthals: we can therefore deduce that there was sexual activity between the two species.

[5]Ian Morris in *Why the West Rules, for Now* (Princeton, N.J.: Princeton University Press, 2010).

invented pottery, the first looms, and architecture.[6] It was the dawn of the "short" time of history. The "deep" time that transformed humans biologically has since scarcely played a role. A few genetic mutations have occurred, such as one enabling the production of lactase, the enzyme that allows us to digest milk products, but these are minor. Jared Diamond mentions one of his Aborigine friends, born in a village straight out of the Stone Age, who had no difficulty integrating first into a society with writing, then a digital society. "In other words," concludes Diamond, "and it is good news, there was no need for a genetic modification for people to learn to read and to fly a plane."[7]

Several theories address the reasons behind the spread of agriculture. The first is that hunter-gatherers adopted agriculture spontaneously because it is more efficient. Advanced technology drove out more rudimentary techniques. Another interpretation posits a more violent sequence of events. Demographic pressure from farmers, whose numbers grew more quickly as a result of better nutrition, eliminated less dense societies, just as *Homo sapiens* may have eliminated the Neanderthals. Māori farmers thus exterminated their hunter-gatherer neighbors the Moriori (in a region of present-day New Zealand). Extinction can occur indirectly as well. Farmers

---

[6]Prior to 50,000 years ago, all the arts of *Homo sapiens* were repeated in the same form. And then, all of a sudden, a tremendous variety emerged. "No fewer than six distinct styles of stone tools [were] in use in Egypt's Nile Valley between 50,000 and 25,000 B.C.E. . . . Humans had invented style," writes Ian Morris in *Why the West Rules, for Now*, p. 61. In the paragraphs that follow, I borrow a number of points presented in this fascinating book.

[7]Interview in French with Jared Diamond, "Inspirons-nous des papous pour mieux vivre dans notre monde moderne," *Les Echos.fr*, May 28, 2014. http://www.lesechos.fr/28/05/2014/lesechos.fr/0203141236721_jared-dia mond——inspirons-nous-des-papous-pour-mieux-vivre-dans-notre-monde -moderne-.htm.

destroy the ecosystem that once sustained the lives of hunter-gatherers: the wild animals flee, wild plants become inaccessible. As far as the Western world is concerned, the scientific consensus seems to be that, during the period of this great change, one European in four was a foreigner, while three in four were locals who changed their way of life. It is likely, however, that the quarter of the population with foreign origins were war chiefs from the Fertile Crescent, who subjugated the other peoples. In all cases, whether by force or persuasion, a form of technological Darwinism was at work. The most powerful technology carries everything in its way.

THE INVENTION OF HIERARCHIES

Hunter-gatherers and the first farming villages were egalitarian. Chiefs did not pass on their positions to their offspring. Important decisions were made collectively, during festivals or religious ceremonies. In his brilliant book *Society against the State*,[8] the anthropologist Pierre Clastres recounts how the Guayaki people of the Amazon rainforest keep a tight rein on the chief's power, conferring on him the right to speak and die first, but never the right to decide.

With the advent of agricultural labor, a "major transformation" came about. Society became hierarchical: chieftaincies appeared, bestowing hereditary power on the leaders, who lived on the surplus provided by the rest of the population. Society organized itself around specialized groups: soldiers, clerks, priests, peasants. The American sociologist Herbert Simon explains that hierarchical

[8] Pierre Clastres, *La société contre l'État* (Paris: Minuit, 1974).

societies are able to create a high level of complexity, simply by repeating several times in identical form the structure of command.[9] Six ranks allow a king who commands ten princes, who each control ten barons, who are in charge of ten knights, who oversee ten tenant farmers, who themselves have ten peasants beneath them, who, in their turn, have ten children, to control a million people. Ultimately, on that model, a hundred thousand people from the top and middle of the hierarchy control a million peasants or slaves at the bottom.

Hierarchies between the sexes also developed. The original division of labor between male hunters and female gatherers became more pronounced with the transition to agriculture. When land was plentiful, men and women cultivated the earth in what was still an egalitarian manner. When demographic pressure increased, fieldwork became more intensive. A good number of women, however, were as strong physically as the average man, and in fact their labor was more arduous. Ian Morris has described the skeletons of 162 residents of the Mesopotamian village of Tell Abu Hureyra, which dates back to an era prior to agriculture. Both women and men had crushed vertebrae at the top of their spines, a sign that they carried heavy loads, but only the women had arthritis in their feet, because they milled grain while sewing. With agriculture, a new arrangement was set in place: men did the outdoor labor, women the indoor. Hunter-gatherer societies favored a certain variety in women's roles, whereas agrarian societies everywhere devalorized women, confining them to a reproductive function.

[9] See, for example, Herbert Simon, "Organisations and Markets," *Journal of Economic Perspectives* 5, no. 2 (1991): 25–44.

THE BIRTH OF EMPIRES

The "West" first invented the agricultural revolution, and kept this advantage for about a millennium and a half. The word "West" here refers to the geographical area originating in the Fertile Crescent. The agricultural revolution that began in 9000 B.C.E. reached Turkey in 8000, Greece in 7000, Italy in 6000, Central Europe in 5000, and France in 4000. It took a millennium for each border to be crossed. Within the Fertile Crescent, Mesopotamia, between the Tigris and the Euphrates rivers, had a unique destiny. That region, which covers present-day Iraq, was hot and humid. The monsoons from the Indian Ocean brought rain, but only in small quantities. It required more than twenty generations to make the transition from an agriculture watered by rains to one irrigated by river water. In about 3800 B.C.E., a (new) cooling of the climate reduced the intensity of the monsoons. Mesopotamia faced the risk of collapse. It dealt with that risk by improving its socioeconomic organization, thanks to an even more complex irrigation system, which made possible the storage of water until the monsoon season.

Gordon Childe uses the term "urban revolution" to characterize the transformation of Mesopotamia in the fourth millennium B.C.E. Uruk, the Athens of its time, was the great metropolis, not only a city but a state with the capacity to levy taxes and mobilize the forces required to impose its authority. The first tablets containing writing belong to that period. Ian Morris, with great brilliance,[10] shows how Uruk became the center of a trade network with Syria, the Nile Valley, and places as far away as the

[10] Morris, *Why the West Rules.*

Iranian plateau. Uruk controlled a hinterland of villages connected to one another by a dense web of canals allowing for the transport to the city of both grain and people. This has been called the "Uruk world system."

It was the same story in Egypt. The decrease in monsoons in 3800 B.C.E. posed the same challenges. In response, in about 3100 B.C.E., the Nile Valley underwent a major political transformation, which led to the greatest kingdom known in that period, comprising a million subjects. The Great Pyramid of Giza, built in about 2500 B.C.E., remained the tallest building in the world (455 feet) until the construction of Lincoln Cathedral in 1311 (525 feet). These two empires, latecomers in the agricultural world, long dominated the Fertile Crescent region, by virtue of a law known to economists as "the advantage of backwardness," articulated by the Russian-born historian Alexander Gerschenkron. Economic "backwardness" is a strength, in that a backward society can devote all its energy to imitating another, without losing its way in the multitude of possible paths.[11]

At the other end of the world, in the Yellow River Valley to the north and the Blue River Valley to the south, the cultivation of rice began between 8000 and 7500 B.C.E., that of millet in about 6550 B.C.E. Agriculture subsequently spread to all the bordering basins, then westward, toward the Wei River and the Qin region. In 3800 B.C.E., a colder and drier climate made the wet valleys of the Blue and Yellow rivers easier to cultivate. The change of climate did not lead to the political discontinuity observed in Egypt and Mesopotamia, but it did create a new force of the same nature, the "hydraulic" empires,

---

[11] Alexander Gerschenkron, *Economic Backwardness in Historical Perspective: A Book of Essays* (Cambridge, Mass.: Harvard University Press, 1962).

which were more organized than those that depended solely on rainwater.

THE EAST AND THE WEST

The two extremities of the Eurasian world would follow the same stages of development, in terms of writing, religion, sacrifices, pottery, the funerary monuments of leaders, labor (increasingly intense for most of the populations), food storage, fortifications, and the domestication of animals such as dogs.

Fifteen hundred years after the West, the East went through the same major phases, though with a few exceptions. Pottery appeared in the East seven thousand years earlier than in the West (a sign, perhaps, that humans in the region ended their nomad life before the invention of agriculture). Conversely, altars dedicated to the gods were built almost six thousand years sooner in the West.[12] But overall, it is the similarities that prevail. According to the English anthropologist Jack Goody,[13] that parallel development should not surprise us. The two ends of the Eurasian world created civilizations that were based on the Bronze Age in about 3000 B.C.E.[14] It

[12] Temples played a decisive role in Mesopotamian development. They were in possession of vast lands and oversaw the redistribution of crops. Residents of Mesopotamia instinctively turned to the priests, relying on their access to the gods to learn what ought to be done (Morris, *Why the West Rules*).

[13] Jack Goody, *The Theft of History* (New York: Cambridge University Press, 2006).

[14] The Bronze Age gave rise to very similar developments: use of the plow and of draft animals, urban artisanry, and the invention of writing. Asia and Europe also share the same dowry system, either in the form of an inheritance upon the death of the parents or as dowries proper at the time of marriage (in contrast to the African system, where the family of the future groom offers goods and services to the bride's family).

is possible, in fact, that the Bronze Age was imported from the West by the East, which would explain why the center of gravity of the first Chinese dynasties was located inland.

The porosity of cultures within the Eurasian zone can be explained by its specific geography. As Jared Diamond points out, Eurasia lies along an east–west axis, whereas the Americas and Africa extend along a north–south axis. By definition, all the regions along an east–west axis have the same latitude, which means they also have the same seasonal variations. Consequently, agricultural inventions propagate at a much more rapid pace. Although southern Italy, Iran, and Japan span a distance of some four thousand miles, agriculture has common climatic conditions in all three places. In the time of Christ, grains from the Fertile Crescent were growing over an area of ten thousand miles, from Ireland to Japan. What could be called Eurasian civilization, in all its unity and diversity, had come into being. By contrast, llamas in the Andes would never arrive in North America, and horses would not cross the barrier of the Sahara to reach the temperate climates of South Africa. The spread of knowledge on continents located along a north–south axis is much more difficult.

A MEASURE OF COMPLEXITY

To analyze the evolution of the East and the West across the centuries, Ian Morris has compiled an index that aggregates several kinds of data, representing across history what GDP tells us about the wealth of contemporary nations. The first parameter selected is the level of energy capture of which a society is capable. The second is its war-making capacity. The rate of urbanization is a third criterion. On each scale, the base number 1,000 is assigned to the all-time record known to have been attained anywhere.[15]

Between the Neolithic Age and 5000 B.C.E., the numbers calculated by Morris's index doubled in the West, and the East followed the same evolution a millennium and a half later. Each of the two civilization blocs reached the same complexity threshold (42/1,000), and neither was able to exceed it. China reached that level of complexity in 1150, at the high point of the Song Dynasty, after which it began to decline, as Roman civilization had done a millennium earlier. Not until the Industrial Revolution in nineteenth-century Europe would that record be surpassed—and shattered.

Given that parallelism between the two edges of the Eurasian world, ought we to conclude that human beings are only passive, unresourceful robots programmed by rain, climate, fauna, and flora? "Of course these fears are misplaced," replies Jared Diamond. "Without human inventiveness, all of us today would still be cutting our meat with stone tools and eating it raw."[16] Diamond notes that a good number of fundamental inventions were made only once. Such was the case for the "water wheel, rotary quern, tooth gearing, magnetic compass, windmill, and camera obscura,"[17] the most ingenious

---

[15]The largest city known is Tokyo: 27 million residents in the year 2000. The Roman Empire in its time had as many as a million residents. The population of Chang'an, China, was half that. Rome therefore receives a grade of (1/27) x 1,000, Chang'an a score smaller by half. In terms of energy expended, the Americans currently hold the record, at 200,000 kilocalories per day. Given that the subsistence threshold for the human body is on the order of 2,000 calories, the lowest score in human history is 10/1,000.

[16]Jared Diamond, *Guns, Germs, and Steel: The Fates of Human Societies* (New York: W. W. Norton, 1998), p. 408.

[17]Ibid., p. 255.

invention of all being the alphabet, which does seem to have appeared only once in all of human history. It can be attributed to speakers of Semitic languages living in a region between modern Syria and the Sinai in the second millennium B.C.E. The hundreds of alphabets that existed or still exist are all derived from that ancestral Semitic alphabet. The alphabet was not "necessary" for agricultural societies: only human ingenuity in all its unpredictability accounts for it, ramified by the formidable capacity of human beings to appropriate ideas from other cultures.

❧

CHAPTER 3

November 13, 2026

In the late eighteenth century, Thomas Malthus described human history in terms of an extremely simple mechanism: when human beings are better nourished, they multiply. Agriculture and the subsequent improvements made to it triggered a population explosion that canceled out the initial benefit of a better diet. According to Malthus, the human population tends to increase exponentially so long as the food supply is adequate, then collapses when the agricultural yield reaches its limit. If, for example, the population doubled every hundred years, within a thousand years it would have multiplied a thousandfold. Yet cultivable lands are cleared at a much slower rate. Population growth is irremediably hampered by the scarcity of farmland. Famines and ecological disaster necessarily put an end to periods of expansion.

In that light, economic history appears to alternate destructively between periods of expansion and crisis. When resources are abundant, the population grows unfettered. When the increasing population runs up against a scarcity of resources, crisis results. But every tendency generates its own countertendencies. Human beings become too numerous, but, by virtue of their very number, they give rise to new ideas that push back the limits of the possible. In 1965 the Danish economist Ester Boserup published an important book titled *The Conditions of Agricultural Growth,*[1] in which she demonstrated that demographic pressure spurs inventiveness, which tends to solve the problems caused by overpopulation. The more human beings, the more ideas, and the more resources: these create a dynamic that mitigates the law of diminishing returns specific to agriculture.

In a pathbreaking article, "Population Growth and Technological Change,"[2] the Harvard economist Michael Kremer demonstrates that the theories of Malthus and Boserup, far from being contradictory, have played out in tandem over the course of history. Human beings reach the limits of their food-producing capacities (Malthus), but just as constantly push back those limits, thanks to the inventiveness brought about by the larger number of individuals (Boserup). Result: the planet is populated by an increasing mass of starving people! According to Kremer's calculations, the population grows not exponentially, as Malthus believed, but even more rapidly. The rate of growth itself increases, as in a nuclear reaction, with the size of the population.

The problem was that the population bomb seemed set to go off at the end of a very finite period of time. One study extrapolated population growth on the basis of observations made over the last ten thousand years.[3] It concluded that the earth's population was scheduled to reach the point of infinity on November 13, 2026.

[1] Ester Boserup, *The Conditions of Agricultural Growth* (Chicago: Aldine, 1965).

[2] Michael Kremer, "Population Growth and Technological Change," *Quarterly Journal of Economics* 108, no. 3 (August 1993): 681–716.

[3] Allen Johnson and Timothy Earle, *The Evolution of Human Societies* (Stanford, Calif.: Stanford University Press, 1987), cited in David Christian, *Maps of Time: An Introduction to Big History* (Berkeley: University of California Press, 2004). Until the Christian era, the population grew at a rate of 0.016 percent per year. Subsequently, the rate of growth would be a hundred times higher.

On the basis of the coefficients calculated by Kremer (who estimated his own parameters independently), that assessment is not far off. The population bomb could be predicted to detonate in the mid-twenty-first century.

We will escape that fate, but only because of a miracle: a demographic change that no one at the time anticipated or understood. First in the industrialized countries, then throughout the world, human beings radically reduced their birth rate. An unpredictable event, the transition from the quantity to the quality of children, in the words of economist Gary Becker, saved humanity from a programmed collapse.

THE ACCURSED SHARE

Was reproduction the outlet that human beings found for the excess of energy that a better diet offered them? So suggests Ian Morris. Georges Bataille, better known for his essays on eroticism, indicates the same thing in *La part maudite* (*The Accursed Share*), approaching the question from a new angle.

For Bataille, the origin of human civilizations lies in a simple principle of energy. "The source and essence of our wealth is provided by sunlight, which dispenses energy—wealth—without asking for anything in return." Just as a herbivore is prodigal when compared to a plant, and a carnivore prodigal when compared to a herbivore, man is, of all living beings, the most apt to consume—intensely, luxuriously—the excess of energy provided by nature. "The history of life on earth," explains Bataille, "is primarily the effect of a mad exuberance: the production of increasingly costly forms of life."

According to him, human societies absorb the energy surplus available to them in an entirely arbitrary way. Population growth is only one modality. The Aztecs, for example, built enormous pyramids, at the top of which they performed human sacrifices. "Their conception of the world was singularly and diametrically opposed to our own, but they were no less preoccupied with sacrificing than we are with working." The victim was a surplus extracted from the mass of useful wealth. Once he was chosen, he became the *accursed share* destined to be violently consumed. In the United States and Canada, the potlatch of the native peoples of the Pacific Northwest exemplifies a situation in which a formal gift of considerable riches, offered by a chief to his rival, is intended to humiliate the recipient, to challenge him and oblige him to reciprocate. "A life of squandering is rewarded by the prestige it brings to the squanderer."

In appearance, the system of the Tibetans was the exact opposite: they did not even feel the need to defend themselves. Their "solution" to squandering the surplus was to give everything left over to the monasteries, thus keeping alive a mass of sterile consumers. Everywhere, sacrifices, feasts, and wars absorb a society's excess energy. The modern world sets aside the surplus for industrial equipment. Bataille concludes: "Societies have no other option but to reach 'everywhere the limits of their possibilities,'" without ever understanding the law that guides them. Population growth is a prime example of Bataille's ideas: it could have led an uncomprehending humankind to a chaotic end.

CHAPTER 4

ॐ

The Invention of Money

Money, like writing, is one of the instruments that set human history on the path toward cumulative growth. It was invented in the kingdom of Lydia in the early sixth century B.C.E. According to Herodotus, the history of money dates back to Gyges, founder of the Mermnad dynasty. A 1646 painting by Jacob Jordaens depicts Gyges hidden behind a curtain, contemplating the naked beauty of the queen, surrounded in a halo of light. She was the wife of Candaules, a king so proud of her beauty that he wanted to show her to his vassal. The queen saw Gyges observing her and offered him the following choice: Kill the king or kill himself for the affront done to her.[1] He chose to kill Candaules. Shortly thereafter, the kingdom of Lydia invented money. Croesus would be the last and most famous representative of that dynasty.

Herodotus, who describes this episode at the beginning of his *Histories*, finds it hard to explain why it was the Lydians and not the Greeks who invented money. The two peoples had the same pastimes. Both played games of all kinds. The Lydians, Herodotus says, "invented many of them during a great famine: one day they would play, one day they would eat." . . . He adds however that "all the daughters of the common people of Lydia prostitute themselves, to earn dowries, until they can get themselves

---

[1]Plato gives a different version. According to him, Gyges was a shepherd who discovered a ring that made him invisible, which allowed him to enter the king's palace, where he seduced the queen.

a husband; which, however, they chose for themselves as well."[2] Might girls choosing prostitution as a means to accumulate a dowry be the ultimate cause of the invention of money? Herodotus suggests so, but he does not linger on the question. What seems most important to him, in the end, is to note that money was invented not that long ago.

Granted, Egypt and Mesopotamia in biblical times were not unfamiliar with "money," which I place in quotation marks, following the practice of Georges Le Rider in his brilliant *La naissance de la monnaie* (*The Invention of Money*).[3] But this "money" was anonymous, gold—or, more often, silver—ingots, which had to be weighed regularly. The state's money, stamped by the king, radically changed the scope of the instrument. It was no longer one commodity among others but the source of a new, universal language.

A NEW LANGUAGE

The anthropological meaning of money has been brilliantly expounded by two French economists, Michel Aglietta and André Orléan.[4] Without money, social relations within societies must necessarily be direct. The communications theorist Paul Watzlawick explains that a cat mewing in front of a refrigerator is not saying, "I

---

[2] Herodotus, *Histories*, with an English translation by A. D. Godley (Cambridge, Mass.: Harvard University Press, 1926), 1.93.

[3] Georges Le Rider, *La naissance de la monnaie* (Paris: Presses Universitaires de France, 2001).

[4] Michel Aglietta and André Orléan, *La monnaie entre violence et confiance* (Paris: Odile Jacob, 2002).

want milk" but rather, "Be mother to me."[5] Likewise, exchanges without the use of money are inextricable from the circle of social relations, which inevitably establish alliances or relations of subordination.

In a monetary relationship, exactly the opposite occurs. A payment in cash concludes a relationship. I pay you, we're even! The anthropologist Gordon Childe believes that the introduction of struck coinage made it possible to escape absolute dependence on the group. I can buy a commodity from a stranger whom I will never see again. In fact, if I think I will never see him again, I must pay him in cash.[6] Adam Smith would say that, thanks to money, there is no need to smile at the baker to get a loaf of bread. Money allows one to free oneself from relationships with other people. From the start, monetary exchanges have walked a thin line. They allow relations among people who do not know one another, but, paradoxically, these networks are never so effective as when they rely on ties of solidarity within a given group.[7]

According to Karl Polanyi, the monetary economy was long "embedded" in society. In his view, the economy did not represent a truly distinct realm until late in its history. Polanyi argues that it was not until the "great transformation" of the nineteenth century that the economy came to be "disembedded" from society. Laurence

[5]Paul Watzlawick, Janet Helmick Beavin, and Don D. Jackson, *Pragmatics of Human Communication: A Study of Interactional Patterns, Pathologies, and Paradoxes* (New York: W. W. Norton, 1967), p. 44.

[6]That is the thesis of John Kareken and Neil Wallace, *Models of Monetary Economies* (Minneapolis, Minn.: Federal Reserve Bank of Minneapolis, 1980).

[7]On this subject, see Avner Greif, *Institutions and the Path to the Modern Economy: Lessons from Medieval Trade* (Cambridge: Cambridge University Press, 2006).

Fontaine, in her beautiful book *L'économie morale* (*The Moral Economy*),[8] shows that, until the seventeenth century, credit was something very different from our understanding of it. You lent to someone who was then in your debt, but you were not always concerned with being reimbursed strictly speaking, even though, in Europe, a commercial revolution was already well under way. Economics as a full-fledged intellectual discipline also emerged belatedly. It was really not until the eighteenth century that the notions that form the basis of economic reasoning—production, investment, annuities, profits—became part of an organized discourse.

Money, in fact, was long marked by a deep distrust toward anyone who used it to elevate himself above his station. In both the East and the West, merchants usually came from modest backgrounds and were for the most part uninvolved with the life of the commonwealth. A *metic* in Athens, a foreigner who was neither a citizen nor a slave, could accumulate considerable wealth, but it made little difference to his standard of living. "As a man debarred from owning land and houses, he could not, for instance, raise horses, give feasts, or erect a mansion. Even the few rich metics led unglamorous lives."[9] For a long time, money would be associated with metics and not pose a potential threat to the traditional order of society.

MONEY AND THE STATE

Markets, however, did not emerge out of nowhere during the Industrial Revolution. Most contemporary historians

[8] Laurence Fontaine, *L'économie morale* (Paris: Gallimard, 2008).
[9] Karl Polanyi, *The Livelihood of Man* (New York: Academic Press, 1977), p. 88.

express reservations about Polanyi's theories. Commerce, whether local or long-distance, quickly came to constitute an important dimension of the societies of antiquity.[10] According to Goody, "traders were important both to the government and to themselves in early urban societies, such as Mesopotamia and Central America. The Akkadian kings intervened on behalf of merchants venturing abroad, while among the Aztecs refusal to trade served as a pretext for an attack."[11] It is an oversimplification to contrast the reciprocity of the *oikos* or domestic economy to mercantile trade. From the Bronze Age onwards one could observe the emergence of cities, artisanship, and a "bourgeoisie" earning their livelihood from commerce. One of the first applications of writing in Mesopotamia, China, and elsewhere was the extension of credit. The widespread idea that property rights were "absent until the advent of Roman law in Europe" neglects other societies. "Written 'contracts' were used in China as 'documents of declaration,' including the transfer of land—and had been since the Tang period."[12]

Money was invented by the state, offering a means to collect taxes otherwise than in kind. For someone who wanted to build a state that could maintain an army and a police force, it was not very useful to be paid in chickens or sheep. The state required money so that, in its own manner, it could shatter relations of reciprocity,

[10]Two types of trade, long-distance and local, have always existed. Local trade is concerned with basic necessities, textiles, and domestic items; long-distance trade, with luxury items (gold, leather, gemstones, slaves), which are the basic necessities of the powerful. The agora and the bazaar are examples of local markets that offered fresh milk and eggs, fish and meat. Long-distance trade was at first carried out by embassies, which engaged in the exchange of gifts, following the conventions of a traditional economy. Trade was often an alternative to raids, with no clear division existing between the two.

[11]Goody, *The Theft of History*, p. 36.

[12]Ibid., p. 70.

composed of gifts and exchanges in kind. It had to have a "universal" means of payment to finance its administration.

THE GRECO-ROMAN WAY

Greece took an original path. In the Athens of Pericles, large landowners provided free meals, but Pericles, in the name of the democratic idea, saw to it that all citizens were granted a subsidy in cash to shop at the markets. He himself sold his entire year's crops all at once and then, little by little, purchased what he needed on the agora. Property owners in ancient Greece did not look down on commerce when it served their own interests. Greece had to import its grains, because the soil of Attica was better adapted to the production of oil and wine. Landowners therefore sold the wine they produced to provide their "manors" with food. This commerce was as crucial in antiquity as the petroleum trade is now for industrialized economies. For that very reason, as Polanyi has pointed out, the trade price was not left to the free market but soon regulated, sometimes by decree. Ironically, in the wake of these exchanges, a vast Mediterranean trade grew up that was not under the control of any one state.[13]

---

[13] Goods flowed into Athens from all sides, as they would later do into London. Polanyi gives a vivid description:

> Chalcidian swords and cups, Corinthian bronzes, Milesian woolens, Argive weapons, garlic from Megara, game and fowl from Boeotia, cheese and pork from Syracuse, grapes and figs from Rhodes, acorns and almonds from Paphlagonia, mustard from Cyprus, cardamom from Miletus, onions from Samothrace, marjoram from Tenedos, wine from Attica, Chios, Cnidus, and Thasos, trumpets from Etruria, chariots from Sicily, luxurious chairs from Thessaly, bedsteads from Miletus,

Then Greece became part of the Roman Empire. In the span of a human lifetime, Rome, a small republic in central Italy, came to control the Mediterranean world and quickly mobilized its resources for its own benefit. Egypt and the Gauls were in charge of the wheat supply; textiles came from the Middle East, amphorae from Greece, metals from Spain.[14] The Romans had no difficulty adopting and generalizing the Greek legacy of money and laws. They themselves were extraordinarily constitutionalist, serious lawmakers who easily integrated Greek commercial law.[15] In Rome, despite the persistence of aristocrats' contempt for commerce—a contempt that was just as tenacious there as it had been in Athens—trade quickly became an integral part of the empire.

Rome is known for the "bread and circuses" it offered the plebeians. Even so, the Roman Empire's civic spending should not mask the fact that its primary expense was its army, which required that taxes be collected in cash. Rome marketed the wheat it received as in-kind payments through middlemen. The monopolies granted to salt and iron were also fiscal strategies by which the state sought to fill its coffers. What in the sixteenth to seventeenth centuries would be called mercantilism—an alliance between merchants and kings against the feudal powers—had been a common practice on the part of states from the start.

Law and money produced a syntax that would prove an invaluable resource for Renaissance Europe, to be used as a compass on its new path toward a trade-governed

---

carpets and pillows from Carthage, incense from Syria, hunting dogs from Epirus. (Polanyi, *Livelihood of Man*, pp. 227–228.)

[14] Cf. Pierre Bezbakh, in *Le monde de l'économie,* April 29, 2003.

[15] John Hicks, *A Theory of Economic History* (Oxford: Clarendon, 1969).

economy. The East and the West, previously on parallel paths, would part ways at that time, at least temporarily. The major reason for that (first) great divergence was the following: in the West, the empire would not survive the barbarian invasions, whereas China would withstand the shock.[16] These circumstances, initially unfavorable, would become the source of the West's later advantage. The crisis allowed it to backtrack and to abandon the path on which the Roman system, poor in technology and based on slavery, had been built.[17]

---

[16] At the beginning of the Christian era, two empires, the Roman and the Chinese, in and of themselves governed half the world. Before the gates of the two empires, the barbarians stood at the ready. They ultimately occupied half of each of the two territories (Western Europe in the case of Rome, the northern part of China), while the other half (Byzantium in the Western world, southern China) remained in the hands of a traditional power. Of the two religions—Christianity and Buddhism—that arose in these periods of unrest, only the first would retain its power. The Tang restoration reestablished Confucianism, the religion of the empire. In the West, Christianity would prosper in place of the vanished empire.

[17] That is the subject of Aldo Schiavone's *The End of the Past: Ancient Rome and the Modern West*, trans. Margery J. Schneider (Cambridge, Mass.: Harvard University Press, 2000).

༓

CHAPTER 5

The Theft of History

For a long time, Western history was described without nuance as extending from the Greece of Pericles to the Europe of Dante and Galileo and then to that of James Watt and Adam Smith. It was said to have embodied the triumphal march of Western man toward freedom and prosperity, in contrast to the Oriental system, where the despot bent everyone else's will to his own and kept the common people in abject poverty. The West alone supposedly possessed the resources—philosophical (Greek), moral (Christian), scientific (Galilean), and economic (those of the bankers of Genoa, Florence, Amsterdam, and London)—which allowed it to invent modernity. According to this narrative, Europe was also credited with having invented love (first courtly, then romantic), self-control, and freedom (in the sense of human rights and parliamentary democracy): in short, the individual in the full sense of the term as we use it today.

When analyzed in detail, this edifice quickly collapses. In fact, Greece and Rome never demonstrated any great technological inventiveness. Slave labor was the foundation of economic activity, which meant that ancient Rome remained at an impasse, incapable of using Archimedes's knowledge for anything but war machines. For a long time, the ancient world's contempt for commerce (and for the minorities to whom it was delegated) occupied the Western imagination, surviving in the Christian prohibition on usury. It would be futile to seek in the Greek or Christian heritage the sources of economic prosperity in the sense it is now understood.

The writings of Jack Goody, Ian Morris, and Amartya Sen have also called into question the notion that love, universalist ethics, and other "individualistic" feelings such as the quest for freedom, were Western "inventions." One has only to read Chinese or Indian literature to be convinced otherwise.

Love and sentimental attachments are sometimes linked to individuality and freedom (the freedom to choose one's partner). According to some historians, they are a recent invention: the courtly love of which the troubadours sang only dates back to the Middle Ages, while, according to Jack Goody, in China at the beginning of the third century B.C.E. *The Book of Odes* appears as the first anthology of love poetry. Unlike in the Christian West, love was not a sin in China or Japan, but rather a value to be celebrated. In the bible Solomon's Song of Songs is also a love song (which has been interpreted allegorically). The genre of love poetry was also widespread throughout the Muslim world (*The Ring of the Dove*, composed by the poet Ibn Hazm in 1022, is one example). Goody concludes: "The idea that it was the troubadours who, for the first time, made love 'not a sin but a virtue' may be correct for medieval Europe; it is certainly unsustainable from a world perspective."[1]

In the same way, the transition from shame to guilt has been presented as one of the distinguishing features of the West. A society governed by shame is sustained by external pressure, the gaze of the other. Guilt supposedly marks the passage toward a society characterized by an internalization of social constraints. According to the

---

[1] Goody, *The Theft of History,* p. 274.

sociologist Norbert Elias, its origin can be located in the West, in the shift from feudalism to the absolutist state. It was during that period that a leap toward civilization is said to have occurred, which would in great part explain the Western miracle. To build his argument, Elias magnificently describes how courtly society "civilized"—pacified—aristocratic mores, which then spread via the bourgeoisie to the other social strata. His narrative has one major weakness, however: in taking medieval violence as the starting point for Western civilization, he quite simply disregards the cycle that Westerners lived through after the fall of Rome. In addition, he provides no comparisons with other civilizations.[2] The sixteenth century, which Elias identifies as the start of the civilizing process in Europe, was in reality the beginning of a formidable period of wars and massacres.[3] According to the historian Robert Muchembled, it was that cycle of extreme violence, which would last until the Thirty Years' War (1618–1648), that would allow the state to definitively acquire the monopoly on legitimate violence.[4] But here as well, there is nothing to prove that this process was unique to Europe.

In China, according to Goody, "the complicated rituals of greeting and of bodily cleanliness, of court constraint

[2]The endemic violence of feudal society was caused by the fall of the Roman Empire. As states acquired armies of mercenaries that put an end to the feudal wars, knights became *more violent* in resposne to the appearance of rivals to their military power.

[3]A sharp-tongued commentator has remarked that the year Elias's work was published—1939—hardly favored the claim of a pacification of the West (see Ian Morris, *War* [Princeton: Princeton University Press, 2014]). A passionate paean to Elias's theory, partly taken up by Morris, can be found in Steven Pinker's *The Better Angels of Our Nature* (New York: Viking, 2011).

[4]This was also a period of regression, when the use of the baths was on the decline. Malthus's idea that only Westerners learned to control their birth rate by delaying marriage has been totally refuted by demographers.

as contrasted with peasant directness—as for example in the tea ceremony, all these present parallels to Europe at the time of the Renaissance."[5] Such developments bear witness to a "civilizing process" that was in every way the equal of that in the West. Once the phases of the historical cycle are taken into account, striking parallels become apparent. Codes of good manners and the emergence of a bourgeoisie that aspired to join the aristocracy existed at both extremities of the Eurasian world.

As Kenneth Pomeranz's writings—and those of the California School of economic history more generally—have demonstrated, from the fourteenth century on, no substantial obstacle, whether philosophical or material, stood in the way of a Chinese transition to capitalism, at least when compared to the situation in Europe. China's agriculture was very efficient and its markets well integrated. As for the labor market, there were no obstacles comparable to those raised by the trade guilds in Europe. Labor performed by women was also more common, the result of a deliberate policy. The eternal question arises, therefore: Why did modern economic growth begin in the West?

THE TRAVELS OF MARCO POLO AND COLUMBUS

To pick up the narrative thread: after the fall of Rome, the West entered a long hibernation period. Upon awakening, it discovered that the rest of the world had carried on without it. The Orient was an object of fascination during the European Renaissance, which got under way in the eleventh

[5] Goody, *The Theft of History*, p. 173.

to thirteen centuries. The travels of Marco Polo inspired Western dreams. Venice would build its prosperity on commerce with the Orient. Italian cities such as Venice, Florence, and Genoa provided the model that later inspired Amsterdam and London. The "Western miracle," according to Fernand Braudel, can be attributed primarily to the urban renaissance. Cities ceased to be the aristocracy's place of residence, becoming what Braudel would call an original model of "free," "autonomous," and "industrious" cities.[6]

Born in Genoa, Christopher Columbus set off to discover a new route to India. If any Eurasian people had discovered America, they too would undoubtedly have succeeded in colonizing it, as England, Spain, and Portugal did.[7] In 1405, for example, Admiral Zheng He was in command of three hundred ships, twenty-seven thousand sailors, and one hundred and eighty doctors, and he led them from Nanjing to Sri Lanka and Africa. Zheng used compasses and had resupply ships filled with potable water. Columbus had only three ships and ninety sailors, no reserves of fresh water, and no compass. Nonetheless, China suspended its voyages: it was not especially interested in discovering a new route to Europe; in fact, rather the reverse was true.

The great inventions that would allow the West to rise again were the compass (to aid navigation), the printing press and paper (to spread knowledge), and gunpowder (to wage wars). All were Chinese. In the fourteenth

---

[6] See however, J. Laurent Rosenthal and R. Bin Wong who have shown that the relative peace that reigned in China explains why Chinese "entrepreneurs" did not feel the need to locate their activities in town, behind protective walls. See their *Before and Beyond Divergence* (Cambridge, Mass.: Harvard University Press, 2011).

[7] By virtue of the superiority of the east–west axis over the north–south axis, according to Jared Diamond's demonstration.

century, in fact, China was very close to an industrial revolution similar to the one that would occur in Europe four centuries later. Under the Song Dynasty of the eleventh and twelfth centuries, China surpassed Rome and, according to Morris, experienced its golden age. New products appeared on the markets: agricultural goods, but also paper, hemp, silk, and mulberry leaves.

But that renaissance would collapse under the influence of an external factor, the Mongol invasion in the thirteenth century. Then, in the sixteenth century, at the end of the Mongol threat, Ivan the Terrible closed the Russian steppe, a highway of sorts between East and West. This was one of the causes of Western expansion. The Mongol invasion was fatal to Chinese industry, which regressed vis-à-vis its position in the fourteenth century, never returning to its earlier pace, despite the restoration of the empire under the Ming. According to Pomeranz, Chinese industrial decline was an accident of geography: the Mongol invasion pushed China's intellectual and political center of gravity southward, whereas its coal reserves—a decisive factor for England—were located in the north.

THE RISE OF THE WEST

It is not courtly love or self-control that explains the rise of the West, but rather the permanent war waged by the great powers of Europe. All were obsessed with the same hegemonic dream: to reconstitute the splendor of Rome. "What is Europe?" asked Leibniz. "A fierce struggle of warring neighbors." The quasi–civil war waged by the European powers in a state of mutual fascination was peculiar to the West. The feudal wars, in which a few barons joined their suzerains on the battlefield forty days a year, gave way to a new kind of war, waged by increasing numbers of mercenary armies. The monarch's need for money spread to society as a whole, as it had done in antiquity. The states, already crippled by what they owed to their mercenaries, would create a financial capitalism designed to absorb a continually growing public debt. This was indeed one of the few contributions to the development of capitalism made by the Europe of that time!

War brought considerable progress in artillery and navigation. That advantage would prove invaluable in the wake of the great explorers' discoveries, when the wars of Europe would be extended to the other continents. Conquering the world proved to be much easier than controlling the rest of Europe. This was the discovery the continent's great powers made in the sixteenth to seventeenth centuries, when the Atlantic replaced the Mediterranean as the new *mare nostrum*.[8]

The French author Antoine de Montchrestien, one of the founders of what would become known as the mercantilist school, coined the term "political economy" during this period. According to members of that school, trade is a continuation of war by other means. Nations need to sell more than they buy, in order to bring as much gold as possible into their territory. Mercantilists sought to demonstrate to the princes that the merchants were their best allies. This was not a new idea, of course; it was familiar to the kings of antiquity. But control over society as a whole would become much more far-reaching.

---

[8] Leibniz continues his analysis of the European powers as follows: "The first frenzy turned outward: for Spain, toward South America; for England and Denmark, toward North America; for Holland, toward the West Indies; for France, toward Africa."

THE PROTESTANT ETHIC AND THE SPIRIT OF CAPITALISM

The great discoveries would accelerate that movement, resulting in a vast commercial system. Asia supplied spices, textiles, and porcelain; America, gold, sugar, and tobacco. And Africa contributed the odious third part of that global trade: it sold slaves in exchange for poor-quality products (compared to those from Asia) provided by Europe. The climactic moment in feudal society's transformation into a mercantile society came in England, with the enclosure movement of the seventeenth century, when English lords did not hesitate to drive the peasants off their fields, so that they could graze sheep there and sell the wool to Dutch weavers.[9] Robert Castel brilliantly describes this period as one when labor became "disaffiliated" from its ancestral bonds and created a new historical experience, a precursor to what would much later become wage labor.[10]

This was an era when John Calvin was almost literally de-demonizing wealth: riches were not the devil's work, he explained, but proof of divine election. Greed was still a sin at the time. Martin Luther himself despised trade and repeated the Catholic Church's traditional condemnation of usury. Calvinist merchants were freed from that prohibition, but they had to observe heaven's

[9]The Dutch Republic shifted Europe's economic geography northward. It organized regular trade with Poland, woolens in exchange for wheat, then gradually extended commerce to Spain and Portugal. The Italian cities, which dominated the textile trade and the credit system in the Middle Ages, gradually lost ground to Dutch competition, whose model was then replicated in England. At first, England was in the commercial orbit of the Netherlands, exporting sheep's wool to be processed by the Flemings, before the wool gradually ascended the value chain.

[10]Robert Castel, *Les métamorphoses de la question sociale* (Paris: Fayard, 1995).

benevolence without taking any personal pride in it: glorifying God meant denying their own glory. They had to "humbly" accept being wealthy.

In a brilliant formulation by R. H. Tawney (quoted by Bataille), Calvin is said to have offered the bourgeoisie of Geneva what Marx offered the proletariat: the promise of a world to come that would belong to them. At the same time Tawney observes that, wherever Calvinism dominated, it imposed a kind of collective dictatorship. Later, with the advent of the English Puritans in the second half of the seventeenth century the (young) tradition would lead to the unfettered pursuit of profit. In 1688, when William of Orange ousted James II (who would take refuge in France), the accord between capitalism and religion, concluded in Geneva, would come to London, forging what Max Weber would interpret as the spirit of capitalism.

The work of Douglas North and his coauthors along with more recent works by Daron Acemoglu and James Robinson have made a convincing case that the "Glorious Revolution" of 1688–1689 was a decisive moment in the rise of modern capitalism, to the extent that it offered a new institutional framework protecting property rights more efficiently.[11] This is certainly a critical step; however, it must be placed in the broader context of the pan-European revolution that England was able to build upon.[12]

[11] North, D., and R. Thomas, *The Rise of the Western World* (Cambridge: Cambridge University Press, 1973); Acemoglu, D., and J. Robinson *Why Nations Fail* (London: Profile Books, 2012).

[12] See however the work by Quinn, which shows that the price of capital was not significantly reduced after the "glorious revolution." Quinn "The Glorious Revolution's effect on British Private Finance: A Microhistory: 1680–1705," *The Journal of Economic History*, vol. 61, no. 3, (2001) pp. 593–615. Jean-Laurent Rosenthal also criticizes the "enclosure" efficiency argument by

THE ADVENT OF MACHINES

If one had to choose a single circumstantial factor responsible for the transformation of the European economy, it would be the Black Death in the fourteenth century. The equivalent, for a feudal system, to the 1929 stock market crash for Western capitalism, it turned the world on its head. The number of peasants dropped radically, reversing —to their advantage—the balance between men and land. The crisis gave peasants the opportunity to escape their servile condition by renting out their services to the highest bidder. Everywhere in Europe, it produced a rise in wages, which would eventually reach twice their usual level.

The freedom from food scarcity would be of short duration, however. Demographic growth quickly resumed, and the population of Europe returned to what it had been before the Black Plague. As the number of people increased, wages began to return to "normal." By the end of the seventeenth century, that process was complete almost everywhere. Two countries, however, were shielded from that ebb tide: England and the Netherlands. Wages there remained close to the highs achieved after the Black Death. The economic historian Robert Allen has shown, for example, that in eighteenth-century England, the common man could buy white bread, beef, beer, and such luxury goods as a mirror, sugar, or tea. In Florence, by contrast, he ate bread in the fifteenth century but, in the eighteenth, could afford only polenta made from corn, recently imported from America.[13]

---

showing that overly tight property rights may have hampered productive investments in agriculture. Jean-Laurent Rosenthal, "The Development of Irrigation in Provence, 1700–1860," *Journal of Economic History*, vol. L, no. 3 (Sept. 1990), pp. 615–638.

[13]Robert Allen, *The British Industrial Revolution in Global Perspective* (Cambridge: Cambridge University Press, 2008).

Several factors account for why wages remained high in the Netherlands and England. Those two countries profited most from the flow of commerce that occurred in the wake of the explorations of the sixteenth and seventeenth centuries.[14] At the same time, they experimented sooner than the rest of Europe with new agricultural technologies—crop rotation in particular—thanks to the new science.

According to Allen, wages as low as those generally found throughout history created no incentive for industrial development: Why mechanize labor when labor cost next to nothing? That attitude, which dug Rome's economic grave (the empire was unable to emancipate itself from slave labor), remained a crucial factor in Europe in the seventeenth and eighteenth centuries. The rupture created by the Black Plague brought about a change in direction. In the mid-eighteenth century, on the eve of the Industrial Revolution, English wages were 60 percent higher than those in France. That situation considerably increased the incentive to mechanize labor.

It would seem, then, that high wages account for the Industrial Revolution rather than vice versa. Allen analyzes one of the machines that was key in the transformation of the English textile industry, the first commercially successful machine for spinning cotton, invented by

[14]The Netherlands and England would dislodge Portugal as Asia's trading partner. The Dutch made Jakarta the capital of the Asian empire after they took it away from the Portuguese. The English in turn created their empire at the expense of the Dutch. Several wars later, the English took New York from the Dutch (in 1664) and settled along the Atlantic coast, from Maine to Georgia. They exported tobacco, rice, and wheat to England. In 1770 the English population of America reached 2.8 million, half as large as the population of England proper. Trade with the colonies would boost the English and Dutch economies. On the eve of the Industrial Revolution, the proportion of the population in England that earned a living through farming had already fallen below 45 percent.

Richard Arkwright. According to Allen's calculations, the return on investment for an Arkwright spinning frame in England was 40 percent. In France, it would have been only 9 percent. Because wages were lower there, it was less profitable to substitute machines for human labor. It would not be until the nineteenth century that these ingenious machines would be improved and that their reduced production cost would make them profitable in countries (such as France) that had lower wages.

The modern world beckoned. Machines had made their appearance, and soon the steam engine would vastly increase the quantum of energy that English industrialists mobilized to run their factories.[15] But what provided the West with its upward thrust and allowed the initial process to intensify instead of waning—as is ordinarily the case—was the scientific revolution, the second Big Bang in human history, which would turn the understanding of the world on its head and would quickly become the driving force of economic life.

---

[15]English and Dutch urbanization had increased the demand for energy. Because the price of wood had gone through the roof, substitute products were sought out: in the Netherlands, peat; in England, coal.

From the Closed World to the Infinite Universe

When Europe awoke from the hibernation that had followed the fall of Rome, it discovered that the rest of the world had continued to progress in the arts and sciences. Arab physicians and philosophers were in the lead. A key moment arrived in 1085 C.E. when the great Islamic city of Toledo fell into the hands of Alfonso VI, king of Castile. A frenzied process of translation into Latin of Greek and Arabic scientific works began at that time. There was an enormous hunger for knowledge. Within two hundred years, that work was completed. Europe was ready to play its part.

Aristotle, rediscovered through Arabic translations, had a paradoxical role in the formation of the European scientific spirit. His philosophy allowed Saint Thomas Aquinas to claim that reason was not the enemy of faith. That opened a breach into which the scientific spirit could insert itself. Aristotle, however, reasoned teleologically: the nature of things is explained by their end result "I have a hand so as to pick an apple," rather than, "I can pick an apple because I have a hand." Aristotle deduced, for example, that heavy bodies must fall faster than light bodies. Not until Galileo dropped a stone from the top of the Tower of Pisa (according to legend) would this belief be shown to be false. Aristotle also thought that an absolute vacuum was an impossibility. Evangelista Torricelli,

Galileo's secretary and disciple, invented the barometer, which measured atmospheric pressure and demonstrated the existence of a vacuum above the mercury column Torricelli was using.[1] The Galilean revolution would thus bring about an unprecedented conjunction between pure reasoning and experimentation. That marriage, as Einstein would say, would be the improbable miracle of modern science.[2]

Paradoxically, the church's 1277 declaration, through the voice of the archbishop of Paris, that a number of Aristotelian opinions were heretical, would liberate thought. Beginning in the fourteenth century, Jean Buridan (who invented the famous paradox of Buridan's ass) and his disciple Nicolas Oresme laid out the principles that would later allow Copernicus to start his own revolution.[3] Aristotle had argued that the universe must rotate around the earth. Buridan challenged him in purely speculative terms. If the contrary were true, he said, things would appear exactly the same to us. And he explained why: if a ship circles another, it is perfectly possible for those on board to believe that the second ship is circling the first. Buridan, however, backed away from

---

[1] Atmospheric pressure was one of the subjects of choice of seventeenth-century scientists. Christiaan Huygens and Otto von Guericke, continuing on the path opened up by Torricelli, showed that, when a vacuum is created in a cylinder, atmospheric pressure will force a piston into it. Denis Papin used these findings to produce the first steam engine in 1675, followed by Thomas Newcomen in 1712 (after twelve years of modifications). James Watt next took up the torch.

[2] The idea that the laws governing nature can be discovered through experimentation would be used to good advantage by industrialists. John Harrison, inventor of the chronometer, had read a treatise directly inspired by Newton's lessons. See Joel Mokyr, *The Gifts of Athena* (Princeton: Princeton University Press, 2002).

[3] In the following paragraphs, I have borrowed the invaluable arguments of Dominique Bourg and Philippe Roch, eds., *Crise écologique, crise des valeurs?* (Geneva: Labor et Fides, 2010).

the conclusion that it is actually the earth that rotates because, he said, an arrow shot into the air would in that case not fall back to the same spot. His student Oresme would explain why that argument is inadequate: the arrow's trajectory is governed by the speed of the earth.

Galileo's and Newton's scientific thinking therefore had its genesis in the Middle Ages. Lynn White, a specialist in that period, caused a heated controversy when he suggested that Christianity accounts for the change.[4] He took issue with the usual position that nothing happened from a scientific standpoint between 500 and 1500 C.E. because of the deleterious influence of Christianity (the idea, for example, that the earth was round, accepted unproblematically by Aristotle, was rejected by the church). White argues, on the contrary, that Christianity, by virtue of the biblical faith in a world created by God, encouraged human beings to seek to understand God by understanding nature. In the Middle Ages, "*Natura, id est Deus.*" Nature is God, she *expresses* laws established by God. Westerners inherited a tradition that the earth is the autograph of God."[5]

Similarly, Pierre Legendre writes that "the Bible functioned with the irresistible power of a founding myth, providing the key to a world to be deciphered. . . . In the West, as everywhere else, we are the children of the past. But since the Middle Ages, in the West that past has announced an imminent revolution."[6] In antiquity, the idea

---

[4]Lynn White, "The Historical Roots of Our Ecologic Crisis," *Science* 155, no. 3767 (March 1967): 1203–1207.

[5]According to James Hannam, the biblical God, unlike the Olympian gods, is not capricious. Nature, which is God's work, is marked by perfection, which allows us to understand it. See James Hannam, *The Genesis of Science: How the Christian Middle Ages Launched the Scientific Revolution* (Washington, D.C.: Regnery, 2011).

[6]Legendre, *Ce que l'Occident ne voit pas.*

that the world had a beginning and an end contradicted the conception of cyclical time. The biblical notion of time diverged from the ancients' understanding. It elevated the role of man, who was considered to be in the image of God. Christianity went even further: God himself was incarnated in a man, his Son. According to Lynn White, Christianity is the most anthropocentric religion in existence. In establishing a separation between man and nature, it made modern science possible and, again according to White, therefore lies at the origin of the current ecological disaster (it should be noted that his article was written in 1967).[7]

But was Christianity as such truly the source of the scientific revolution? The Orthodox Church in the East did not take the same path as Christianity in Western Europe. For Descartes, Galileo, and Newton, nature is *not alive*; rather, it is like a machine, which man can operate in the manner of a mechanical clock. That thinking is inconceivable within the Orthodox tradition, which sees God as fully present in the world in a very real way. He is perceptible by the spirit, the *noũs*, which according to the church fathers is a superrational faculty that allows human beings to accede to the ultimate reality of things.[8]

---

[7]Philippe Descola dates the sources of the Western division between nature and culture much further back in history: see his *Au-delà de nature et culture* (Paris: Gallimard, 2005).

[8]The Chinese, who had a clear advantage over the West in the areas of industrial and agricultural technologies, did not abandon their understanding of the universe as being inhabited by a spirit (*qi*) and refused to imagine it was constructed like a clock (see Bourg and Roch, eds., *Crise écologique, crise des valeurs?*). This was not from lack of interest in Western ideas. In 1644, when the Manchus conquered Beijing, the Jesuits won a public competition to predict the next eclipse. The young Kangxi emperor, who came to power in 1668, set about studying arithmetic, geometry, and engineering for several hours every day. But the effort was a failure. The pope worried that the Jesuits were promoting astronomy more than Christianity and placed them under surveillance. The emperor became vexed, opened his own academy, and the bond was broken. Conversely, after the Meiji revolution of 1868, Japan would

As in the case of capitalism, it would be pointless to reduce the scientific revolution to an intuition that emerged fully formed from seventeenth-century Europe. The Greeks mastered Ptolemy's astronomy but never applied it to a useful purpose—navigation, for example. They thought it was possible to understand the movement of the stars but not the trajectory of a stone.[9] "The possibility of recognizing the sensible world as a territory of reason, of dominating and controlling it by means of experimental verification," eluded Greek and Roman thought.[10] At the other extremity of the Eurasian world, the Chinese developed a far-reaching science, which has been analyzed in detail in the seven dense volumes published by Joseph Needham.[11] But that science tended to be oriented toward the solution of practical problems. The improbable marriage Einstein spoke of, between pure reasoning and experimentation, may owe a great deal to the connection between these two traditions. The West contributed its personal obsession, the belief in the world of ideas, and the East its pragmatism in understanding the world in technical terms.

FROM DIVINE HOPE TO THE IDEA OF PROGRESS

The scientific revolution brought about a shift in the conception of the universe, which was henceforth considered

---

assess the reforms needed to catch up to the West and would make education a priority: in 1890, two-thirds of the boys and one-third of the girls were receiving a complete primary education.

[9] Roger-Pol Droit, *L'Occident expliqué à tout le monde* (Paris: Le Seuil, 2008).

[10] Schiavone, *The End of the Past*.

[11] Joseph Needham, *The Grand Titration: Science and Society in East and West* (London: Allen & Unwin, 1969).

a mathematical space, infinite and void. In his important book *Du monde clos à l'univers infini* (*From the Closed World to the Infinite Universe*), Alexandre Koyré would say that it led to a profound revolution of the human mind, or at the very least the European mind, in that it modified the foundations and the very parameters of our thought.[12] "Some will speak of a crisis of European consciousness, others of the secularization of consciousness, the substitution, for the preoccupation with the next world, of interest in this one. . . . The historians of philosophy will place the emphasis on man's discovery of his essential subjectivity. The literary historians will describe the despair and confusion that the new philosophy brought to a world from which all coherence had disappeared and in which the heavens no longer proclaimed the glory of God."

The *Grand Siècle*, as the seventeenth century is called in French, was riddled with doubts and anxiety. What is a human life worth if it is deprived of divine hope? Paul Hazard, in the 1935 book to which Koyré was alluding, *La crise de la conscience européenne* (literally, "The Crisis of European Consciousness," published in English under the title *The European Mind*), indicates the speed at which, within a few decades (between 1680 and 1715), the change in European thinking occurred.[13] "Most French people thought like Bossuet; then, all of a sudden, they thought like Voltaire. The most commonly received ideas, the universal consent that proved the existence of God, the belief in miracles, were called into doubt. The divine was relegated to the unknown and

---

[12] Alexandre Koyré, *Du monde clos à l'univers infini* (Paris: Gallimard, 1962).

[13] Paul Hazard, *La crise de la conscience européenne, 1680–1715* (Paris: Fayard/Le Livre de Poche, 1994).

impenetrable heavens; man and man alone became the measure of all things. For a civilization based on the idea of duty, the 'new philosophers' tried to substitute a civilization based on the idea of law: the laws of individual consciousness, the laws of critique, the laws of reason, the laws of man and of the citizen."

It was in the eighteenth century that the philosophers of the Enlightenment found a way out of the void that had been created in the previous century, by adopting a new faith—progress—which took the place of the Christian hope for redemption to come. In place of the idea of a mythic golden age during which men led an existence close to the gods, without toil or sorrow, the Enlightenment put forward a similar ideal, but as a possible future. According to Frédéric Rouvillois, "most religions of the Book contain the idea of a golden age, a paradise, or a natural garden from which, one day, humanity had to be exiled. Such an idea explains why eyes were turned toward the past, and, in some cases, toward the hope of a new beginning. . . . It is only since the Enlightenment and the spread of secularization that the world has been ruled by the idea of moving forward to something different, something about which one dared not dream."[14]

Montesquieu explains that man, in moving away from the original golden age, lost his simplicity and frugality, his natural innocence, freedom, and equality, but that law and reason can restore that vanished virtue to him. Montesquieu's optimism bursts forth when he declares: "In the state of nature, men are truly born into equality, but they cannot remain there. Society leads them to lose that equality, and they become equal again only through

[14]Frédéric Rouvillois, *L'invention du progrès, 1680–1730* (Paris: Centre National de la Recherche Scientifique, 2010).

laws." The German poet Hölderlin expresses the same idea: "There are two ideal states: extreme simplicity, where, by the mere fact of nature's organization, without our having any part in it, our needs are in harmony with one another; and extreme culture, where the same result is achieved, thanks to the organization that we are able to bestow on ourselves."[15]

For Montesquieu and Rousseau, rational law or the social contract must take the place of arbitrary laws. Man's eternal quest, which is to find his place among other men—the reconciliation, in Hegel's terms, of the "singular and the universal"—reaches its destination when everyone knows he is obeying laws that are just, because based in reason. The Cartesian hope for a science that would allow man to be, "as it were, master and possessor of nature," culminates in a science where man also becomes master and possessor of the society in which he lives.

But none of these authors imagined that man would progress by means of material wealth. Rousseau, concurring with Montaigne, warns in *Émile* that "poverty does not consist of the privation of things but of the need one feels for them." On the whole, Enlightenment thinkers remained wary of the idea of material progress, as Aristotle had been of money. In the eighteenth century, despite the Calvinist revolution, greed was still considered a vice, though it was sometimes also recognized as a good, inasmuch as it turned men away from violence (Montesquieu's major idea).

Even Scottish Enlightenment thinkers, including the eminent moral philosopher and economist Adam Smith,

---

[15] Quoted in Charles Taylor, *Hegel and Modern Society* (Cambridge: Cambridge University Press, 1979).

while they praised markets as a principle of social organization, did not link them to the idea of progress in the moral sense that they understood the term. The notion of perpetual growth had not yet been elaborated. Montesquieu attributed wealth to factors such as climate. According to Adam Smith, the age he was living in had to move toward (and remain in) a new phase of economic development: the Age of Commerce, which came in the wake of three earlier stages—namely, the Age of Hunters, the Age of Shepherds, and the Age of Agriculture.[16]

Smith was preoccupied with the risk of negative consequences that the specialization of labor posed for working-class morality. "This dexterity at his own particular trade seems, in this manner, to be acquired at the expense of his intellectual, social and marital virtues." And, to fend off the moral risk, he recommends the creation of a universal public school system. Smith may have intuited that industrial society would propose something quite different from a transition from an agrarian and authoritarian society to a society of commerce and tolerance. And in fact, it was preparing to create its own world, very remote from the one that the peaceful merchants of Geneva had imagined.

THE DAWN OF THE MODERN WORLD

For a long time, the Industrial Revolution that began in England in the last third of the eighteenth century was

---

[16]Smith chose the famous example of a French pin factory—not exactly the leading edge of technology—to illustrate his idea of the division of labor, even though he had the English textile industry before his eyes. The steam engine is also not cited, but, in fact, the most famous prototype was developed the year *The Wealth of Nations* was published.

described as a unique event, linked to the improbable circumstances that favored it: enclosures, Protestant ethics, etc. However reassuringly familiar this way of thinking is, it is more accurate to see modern economic growth as the product of the long maturation process of human history, in both space and time. Growth, in its different forms, has been a feature of mankind from the very beginning. The sheer fact of language allows humans to accumulate knowledge in ways inaccessible to other species. All the key inventions, from money to writing to printing, allowed mankind to set up a process of knowledge accumulation. It is true, a number of civilizations stalled, some even disappeared, but the strength of the overall process was such that world population kept growing, and would have run into a wall, if it had continued along its previous trends.

What makes the modern world different from previous civilizations are two critical factors. One is the scientific revolution which allowed human knowledge to enter a new phase of acceleration. The other one was the demographic transition that set the dynamics of population growth on a different course. Both are now affecting the entire planet. Time is accelerating everywhere, some might say running out. And it is on board that speeding train that humanity must confront the new challenge posed by the world's finite resources.

PART II

The Future, the Future!

CHAPTER 7

❧

The Singularity Is Near

"The nineteenth century, which began with sailing ships and candles, ended with ocean liners, automobiles, and telephones. In the early twentieth century, women often died in childbirth, children in infancy; tuberculosis was still a death sentence. Hygiene, housing conditions, work, and education were in a deplorable or nonexistent state." As Aldo Schiavone, a specialist in antiquity, summarizes it, the list of inventions credited to the last century is beyond belief: "Radio, radar, television, atomic energy, electrical appliances, transistors, moon landings, mass tourism, digital photography, high-definition television, the Internet, video games, Web 2.0, X-rays, anesthesia, sulphanomides, aspirin, antibiotics, the Pill, chemotherapy, organ grafts, genetic engineering, the Human Genome Project."[1]

Before 1750, the increase over time in per capita revenue was small, even nonexistent. By 1850, nothing was the same. Europeans broke through the threshold (as measured by Ian Morris) that had stopped the Romans and the Song, rising from 40 to 90 on the wealth index and leaving other civilizations far behind. The Netherlands in the eighteenth century, England in the nineteenth, and the United States in the twentieth were by turns the pioneers of their era. At every stage, the rate of economic growth kept increasing: 0.5 percent in the eighteenth century, 1 percent in the nineteenth, 2 percent

---

[1] Aldo Schiavone, *Storia e destino* (Turin: Giulio Einaudi Editore, 2007).

in the twentieth. Could the growth rate double again in the twenty-first century, reaching 4 percent? In view of Michael Kremer's data on population growth, a continuous rise in the growth rate is an appealing hypothesis. It is defended by theorists of so-called "endogenous growth," who believe that a self-perpetuating mechanism of the same nature as in demography is now at work in the production of wealth, leading to exponential growth.[2]

Ray Kurzweil, a futurist who taught at MIT, has radicalized the idea of expanding wealth. Time, he says, is constantly accelerating, and always has been.[3] Every major stage of human history arrives ten times faster than the previous one. If we round off the numbers, hominids appeared ten million years ago, *Homo erectus* a million years ago, *Homo sapiens sapiens* a hundred thousand years ago, agriculture ten thousand years ago, the printing press a thousand years ago, electricity a hundred years ago, and the Internet ten years ago.[4] The major stages of human progress—fire, stone implements, agriculture—took several thousand years to develop. Printing took more than a century. Smartphones have taken over the planet within a decade.

In Kurzweil's opinion, the next stage will begin in 2020, when computers will be able to pass the Turing test: that is, a human being will be unable to distinguish whether she is addressing a computer or another human being. Electronic circuits are a million times faster than the electrochemical circuits used by the human brain. According to Kurzweil, the exponential growth of technologies

[2] The main theorists of endogenous growth are Paul Romer, Robert Lucas, Philippe Aghion, Peter Howitt, Elhanan Helpman, and Gene Grossman.

[3] Ray Kurzweil, *The Singularity Is Near* (New York: Viking, 2005).

[4] As we have seen, hominids actually appeared seven million years ago, *Homo erectus* a million and a half years ago; the Chinese invented printing in 868 C.E. and Gutenberg reinvented it in 1450 C.E.

will soon make it possible to simulate the brain perfectly. There will come a time when all the memory contained in the brain can be stored on a USB flash drive. We will be able to "save" our memory, change bodies (perhaps), and subsequently recover our consciousness.[5] Later on, all of human intelligence will be storable. That will be the singularity. Human intelligence will saturate the universe.

Kurzweil predicts nothing less than an abrupt shift in the human species in 2060. Nanotechnologies will allow "nanobots" (robots at the molecular level) to reverse aging. "Just as there are stem blood cells that will always produce blood cells, or stem muscle cells, we are discovering that there are stem neural cells. There is a potential for regeneration of the brain, for the preservation of at least a fraction of our population of neurons." According to Kurzweil, a transhuman world is coming into being. His predictions are in agreement with those of Craig Venter, a specialist in genetic research and the founder of Celera Genomics. When Venter was criticized for "playing God," he is said to have replied, "We're not playing."

The Defense Advanced Research Projects Agency (DARPA) of the U.S. Department of Defense, which was responsible for the creation of the Internet, takes the transhumanist project very seriously. It launched its Brain-Computer Interface Project, aimed at building computers from DNA molecules instead of silicon, so that they could be implanted in soldiers' brains. A project financed by the National Science Foundation promises network-enabled telepathy, which could be available by 2020. Furthermore, DARPA issued the Robotics

---

[5]This is obviously not the same thing as immortality. Imagine that all your knowledge and emotions are recorded in a large book. The person who reads it will inherit your "self," but you will not survive as a result.

Challenge to the scientific community: develop a robot capable of driving a car, removing debris in front of an entryway, climbing a ladder, closing a valve, and flipping a switch.

Those working in the fields designated by the abbreviation NBIC (nanotechnology, biotechnology, information technology, and cognitive science) are in search of the Holy Grail that will allow doctors to detect genetic diseases in advance and to provide the appropriate treatments. Peter Thiel, co-founder of PayPal, invested part of his fortune in these technologies. Bill Gates, moreover, is fascinated by research on prostheses (he generously donated much of his fortune to a foundation whose resources in the health field are greater than those of the World Bank).

PERPETUAL GROWTH

Theorists of "endogenous growth" are fond of citing Kurzweil's claims because they perfectly illustrate their own expansionist theories.[6] Moore's Law (named after Gordon Moore, cofounder of Intel), according to which

---

[6]The acceleration of economic growth, like that of population in the past, is the chief evidence endogenous growth theorists present. They note that, for the eleven richest countries, between 1700 and 1978 the probability that growth would increase from one decade to the next was always above 50 percent (close to 70 percent in France and the United States). In this vein, the economist William Nordhaus, in a telling example, has calculated the reduction in the cost of lighting. Between 38,000 B.C.E. and 1750 C.E., in the transition from lighting based on animal fat or plant oils to kerosene, the cost of illumination dropped only 17 percent total. The use of candles and whale oil reduced the price by 87 percent in the early nineteenth century, a rate of improvement of 0.06 percent per year. Between 1800 and 1900, the rate was eighteen times higher, 2.3 percent annually, thanks to the carbon-filament bulb. In the twentieth century, as a result of fluorescent lighting, the progress was 6.3 percent per year.

the power of microprocessors doubles every eighteen months, has now taken the place of Malthus's theory of population growth as one of the fundamental laws of economics. It was articulated in an article in *Electronics Magazine* (Moore's original prediction in 1965 was that this power would double every year). That brings to mind a legend cited by Kurzweil concerning the invention of chess in the sixth century, under the reign of a Gupta emperor in India. By way of congratulations, the emperor asked the inventor what sort of reward he desired. The inventor replied that he wanted the chessboard to be covered with grains of rice, one grain on the first square, two on the second, four on the third, and so on (in mathematical terms, the result would be $2^{64} - 1$, which is to say, 1.84×10^{19}).

As Kurzweil indicates, the request seemed reasonable until the midpoint of the chessboard: on the thirty-second square, the emperor provided four billion grains of rice, a value corresponding to the production of an ordinary rice field. It was when he came to the second half of the board that the emperor understood his defeat: he was ruined, no human power could honor his promise. In some versions of the story, the inventor was beheaded. According to Erik Brynjolfsson and Andrew McAfee, who take up the anecdote in *The Second Machine Age*,[7] we too have come to the second half of the chessboard in a world of infinite potential, whose magnitude we have not been able to measure any better than the emperor did.

Brynjolfsson and McAfee's long-term investigation demonstrates the potential of the innovations under way. The information revolution made possible credit cards,

[7] Erik Brynjolfsson and Andrew McAfee, *The Second Machine Age* (New York: W. W. Norton, 2014).

fully automatic wireless telephones, flat screens, and Apple products. A farmer used to push a plow behind a horse; now he drives a tractor guided by GPS. Computers are placed in the service of law firms to examine legal documents. BlackStone Discovery, a Palo Alto company, offers to analyze a million and a half documents a month, for a fee of $100,000. Translation into foreign languages is another area where spectacular progress is being made. The firm GeoFluent, using a technology developed by Lionbridge and IBM, seems to have crossed the threshold of linguistic complexity. Ninety percent of users declared they were delighted with the results. In an entirely different field, IBM produced a supercomputer that defeated its human competitors on the game show Jeopardy!, where contestants must find the question corresponding to a given answer.

As we approach the second half of the chessboard, computers are becoming ever more powerful. Google seems determined to put its stamp on future technologies. The French daily newspaper *Le Monde* sums up the research conducted by the firm: "Contact lenses that measure the level of sugar in diabetics' tears, a spoon that adjusts for the tremors of those suffering from Parkinson's disease, nanoparticles to track cancerous cells: Google aspires to be on the cutting edge of personalized medicine. The medicine of the future is a continuous monitoring of patients' data, according to Andrew Conrad, director of Google X, the experimental facility of Google Life Sciences."[8] A headline on the cover of *Time* asked: "Can Google Solve Death?"

---

[8] Chloé Hecketsweiler, "'La médecine du futur, c'est le suivi continu des données' du patient," *Le Monde*, April 24, 2015, http://www.lemonde.fr/economie /article/2015/04/24/andrew-conrad-patron-de-google-life-sciences-la-medecine -du-futur-c-est-le-suivi-continu-des-donnees-du-patient_4622055_3234.html.

Google glasses offer a simpler example of the new objects to come. They display a constantly visible screen (located at a virtual distance of 2.5 meters) on which to read e-mail, news, and GPS coordinates. Google even promises a model with corrective lenses. More than a gadget that will allow users to see on a new support images already ubiquitous on screens of every kind, Google glasses will let wearers know everything about the person they are addressing: police record, personal data, emotions. The possibilities appear similar to what happens in the dystopian movie *Minority Report* by Steven Spielberg. In October 2010, Google announced that it had fitted out a driverless Toyota Prius and had sent it onto American highways. The car covered more than 200,000 kilometers without mishap. Google put to use the vast quantity of data available on Google Maps and Google Street View. The only incident was when the computer-driven vehicle collided with a car whose driver had braked abruptly at a green light.

Paul Romer, one of the pioneer of "endogenous growth" theories, sums up his optimism as follows: "Every generation has perceived the limits to growth that finite resources and undesirable side effects would pose if no new recipes or ideas were discovered. And every generation has underestimated the potential for finding new recipes and ideas. We consistently fail to grasp how many ideas remain to be discovered. The difficulty is the same one we have with compounding. Possibilities do not add up. They multiply."[9] Even if we concede that a new idea is very often a recombination of old ideas, the possibilities are infinite. Hence Romer calculates that the number of

---

[9] Paul Romer, "Economic Growth," Library of Economics and Liberty Web site, http://www.econlib.org/library/Enc1/EconomicGrowth.html.

possible combinations in a fifty-two-card game is equal to 8.06×10^{67} (= 52!, or 52 factorial in mathematical language), that is, the number of atoms in our galaxy.

To borrow a phrase from Joel Mokyr, an economic historian enthusiastic about the new technologies, the digital revolution is reinventing invention itself.

> Huge searchable databanks, quantum chemistry simulation and highly complex statistical analysis are only some of the tools that the digital age places at science's disposal. The consequences are everywhere, from molecular genetics to nanoscience to research in Medieval poetry. . . . But what is happening to materials now is a leap far beyond any of the past, with new resins, ceramics and entirely new solids designed in silico (that is, on a computer) developed at the nanotechnological level. These promise materials that nature never dreamed of and that deliver custom-ordered properties.[10]

Mokyr does not hesitate to speak of a new Bronze or Iron Age. We have come a long way from the craft apprenticeship that allowed William Perkin to discover by chance an artificial dye, mauveine, or Henry Bessemer to invent (in 1856, the same year as Perkin), the steel manufacturing process that bears his name. Galileo's telescope and Louis Pasteur's microscope, Mokyr announces, now seem to belong to the Stone Age. And Mokyr concludes: "Secular stagnation, not in your life."

---

[10] Joel Mokyr, "What Today's Economic Gloomsayers Are Missing," *Wall Street Journal*, August 8, 2014, http://www.wsj.com/articles/joel-mokyr-what -todays-economic-gloomsayers-are-missing-1407536487.

ϖ

Whither Human Labor?

New technologies primarily focus on the digitalization of tasks that in the past were carried out by humans. Digitalization advances like an incoming tide, engulfing jobs and upending business operations. How far will it go?

In 2004 Frank Levy and Richard Murnane published an important book, *The New Division of Labor*, in which they consider the share of human and digital labor that might exist in the future. Their analysis is based on what is known as "Moravec's paradox," which stipulates that the physical activities that survive digitalization are those that require good sensorimotor coordination. It is fairly easy for computers to pass tests requiring high intelligence (playing chess, for example), but very difficult for them to match a two-year-old hitting a ball. The tasks we know how to do automatically, such as breaking an egg against the side of a bowl, are infinitely more difficult to code than a chess game.

According to Hans Moravec, that paradox could be the result of evolution: millions of years were required for human beings to acquire an advantage in the realm of the senses and perception, whereas the progress in mathematical reasoning occurred much more recently and is therefore much easier to reproduce. In a stunning turn of history, the comparative advantage of man against machine would thus lie in the qualities with which human beings, in their earliest days, prevailed over their primate cousins. According to that line of reasoning, computers push human beings toward tasks where spontaneity and creativity are essential, whereas the electrical age and assembly-line work required exactly the opposite skills.

In an often quoted report, Carl Benedikt Frey and Michael A. Osborne have argued that 47 percent of jobs are threatened by computerization.[1] According to their provocative study, it is the intermediate occupations that are in peril: those of accountant, auditor, vendor, realtor, secretary, pilot, economist, medical staff. The least-threatened jobs are those of psychoanalyst, dentist, athlete, member of the clergy, and writer. There are no digital novelists, the authors reassure us, because human beings will for a long time yet continue to produce fictions on their own. To illustrate this point, Frey and Osborne raise the question of a computer's capacity to make up a good joke. For a computer to produce a subtle witticism, it would need a huge catalogue of jokes already in existence and an algorithm allowing it to discard those that make no sense. For the moment, that does not seem possible. Likewise, tasks that require social or emotional intelligence are nowhere near the point of being computerized. "The scanning, mapping and digitalizing of a human brain . . . is one possible approach . . . but is currently only a theoretical technology."[2] The authors reassure us: even if a large number of nonroutine tasks can be digitalized, thanks to enormous databanks, tasks that require a combination of perception and manipulation, or a creative, social, or emotional intelligence are for the moment protected from computerization.[3]

[1] Carl Benedikt Frey and Michael A. Osborne, "The Future of Employment: How Susceptible Are Jobs to Computerization?" Oxford Martin School, September 17, 2013.

[2] Ibid., p. 27.

[3] The famous battle between Kasparov and Deep Blue is now without interest: the computer wins every time. But the freestyle competition remains inter-

THE MIDDLE CLASS ADRIFT

Most people in the past people tended to assume that it was manual labor jobs, those carried out by the working classes in factories and elsewhere that were most likely to be automated and replaced. Now perhaps counter-intuitively it is the middle classes that are seen as the key segment of the population to be affected by the rise of information and communication technologies.[4] Administrative tasks, the monitoring of other people's work, and middle management are areas in which computers surpass human beings. To make that point, David Autor has broken down American jobs into three categories. Level 1 is composed of managers, "professionals," and high-skilled technicians. Level 2 is made up of jobs situated in the middle of the social hierarchy, those of foreman, administrator, skilled worker. Level 3 comprises the lowest-paying jobs, primarily in personal service and food preparation.

His conclusions? Between 1999 and 2007, just before the Great Recession that followed the subprime lending crisis, level-3 jobs recorded a two-digit growth rate. It was jobs in the middle that were lost. They dropped from 60 percent of all employment in 1970 to 45 percent in 2012. That phenomenon is not specific to the United States. Another study has shown that, between 1993 and 2010, the number of jobs in that category dropped 9

---

esting. The best team is not the top player paired with the best computer, but (according to Kasparov) a pair of good amateurs playing with three computers at once. The matter at hand is no longer to fight against the machine but with it. See Tyler Cowen, *Average Is Over* (New York: Penguin, 2013).

[4]The construction sector provides an example of the limits to the substitution of machines for workers. Workers benefit from computer-assisted technologies in building houses, but, in the end, the human eye and human judgment remain indispensable.

percent in France, 10 percent in Denmark and the United Kingdom, and 7 percent in Germany.[5] During the Great Recession, it was level-2 jobs that experienced the weakest growth, even negative growth in some countries. Autor's analysis is therefore radical: it is not so much the demand for unskilled labor that is falling as that for the intermediate occupations. The middle class arose in the wake of the bureaucratization (private as well as public) that accompanied the development of industrial society. Digital innovations, partly in response, are engineering an enormous cost-cutting operation on those jobs.

The fact that level-3 jobs are gaining ground might lead us to conclude that remuneration for them should be increasing as well. Yet the downward pressure exerted by the failing level-2 jobs prevents such an increase. At the other end of the scale, the meteoric rise in the salaries of the wealthiest 1 percent has produced few countertrends in employment. Why do not at least some level-2 wage earners succeed in rising to level-1 jobs, which are the best remunerated?

A first response might be that it takes time for new cohorts of students to apply in large numbers for the best jobs. In the United States, such applications were surprisingly few in number, perhaps because level-2 jobs had fallen off, which sent contradictory signals to students who might have wished to pursue their studies. But another explanation lies in the notion of winner-takes-all. In postindustrial society, the modes of remuneration tend to give everything to the best and nothing to the second best. The star system, analyzed in the early 1980s by Sherwin Rosen in the United States and by Françoise Benhamou

[5] Maarten Goos, Alan Manning, and Anna Salomons, "Explaining Job Polarization: Routine-biased Technological Change and Offshoring," *American Economic Review* 104, no. 8 (August 2014): 2509–2526.

in France, is also called the "Pavarotti effect": Why purchase an album by anyone besides the best artist? The same phenomenon can be observed everywhere, regarding museums, books, athletes, doctors, lawyers, business owners. A society of superabundant information creates an economy based on reputation that disproportionately increases the remuneration of the person considered to be the best. Whatever the exact mechanism, the result is irrevocable. At both extremes of the employment world, a tremendous asymmetry is created: salaries rise at the top and the number of jobs rises at the bottom, with stagnating wages. The middle class, situated between the two, is falling.

CHAPTER 9

༃

Vanishing Growth?

The world is becoming all-digital, just as it was once all-electric. Yet the central paradox of our time is the following: the promise of the digital revolution is not reflected in statistics on economic growth. In the developed countries, per capita growth continues to fall. In Europe in the last thirty years, it has dropped from a rate of 3 percent in the 1970s, to 1.5 percent in the 1990s, to 0.5 percent between 2001 and 2013.[1] In the United States, 90 percent of the population saw zero growth over the same period.[2]

Technologically speaking, however, the path already traveled is considerable. When the first office computers were introduced, secretary pools were typing thousands of error-free pages, work that is now completely obsolete. Computer data was stored on punch cards. Music was recorded on LPs, and no one could have imagined that several thousands of songs could be available

---

[1] (Weighted) average for France, Germany, and Italy, data from the Organisation for Economic Co-operation and Development (OECD).

[2] Between 1980 and 2010, the income growth for 90 percent of the poorest families was actually negative, dropping from \$33,500 to \$31,600 (adjusted for inflation, and despite the rise in the number of working women). See Emmanuel Saez, http://eml.berkeley.edu/~/saez/TabFig2013prel.xls, income growth table. The median income (that is, the income for the household situated in the exact middle of the distribution) virtually stagnated during the period (+ 0.1 percent increase per year on average). When contributions to health costs are taken into account, the median income rose 0.4 percent per year. See "Economic Report to the President, Council of Economic Advisers," 2015.

on something the size of a matchbox. Letters were sent through the mail, and the reply came several days later. If you were expecting an important call, you had to stay by the phone. Measured against these transformations, even the 1980s looks like the Stone Age. Nevertheless, the period since the advent of the first IBM PC has not been particularly stellar economically. For the vast majority of the developed countries, income stagnation has been the rule.

The economist Robert Gordon has spearheaded an intellectual crusade against the expansionist ideas of "endogenous growth" theorists.[3] He notes ironically that none of the major changes heralded by the science fiction of the 1950s and 1960s have come to pass. We do not travel in personal aerocars, there is no teleportation, we do not live on Mars. When compared to the extraordinary innovations of the previous century, only smartphones appear to be as radical as the earlier revolutionary inventions. For Gordon, the Internet bubble was a unique event, whose effects have already dissipated. "Life is more pleasant, and we have more things to consume, but the speed of material progress has slowed relative to that of the two or three preceding generations."

Gordon strongly makes the case that the exuberant growth of the twentieth century will not be repeated in the twenty-first. Citing the example of transportation, he notes that, since 1958, the speed of travel has stagnated, even regressed. Airplanes fly no faster than they did forty years ago. They consume less fuel and make less noise, but that simply means that they are alleviating the

---

[3] Economic growth is the subject of Robert Gordon's *Rise and Fall of American Growth: The American Standard of Living since the Civil War* (Princeton: Princeton University Press, 2016).

pollution they themselves caused. That is not the same thing as satisfying a new need.[4]

According to Gordon, the computerization of society produced a major but short-lived leap. From the consumer's standpoint, the major inventions revolve around the personality of Steve Jobs and his iPod, iPhone, and iPad series. They are beautiful, miniaturized, and fun, but their importance cannot compare to that of the inventions that preceded them. It took nearly a century for the growth potential of the two industrial revolutions to run dry, but the potential of the computer revolution may be exhausted much more quickly. Hence Gordon's provocative proposal: the idea of growth, in the twentieth-century sense of mass consumption, is disappearing before our eyes, though we are not yet ready to admit it.

In fact, if we look at the major changes in consumption over the last fifty years, we find no overwhelming transformation. In the case of the United States, the most significant change is the change in the cost of food and beverage items, falling from 19.4 percent of total spending in 1959 to 7.8 percent in 2009, and the rise of health service costs, from 5.9 to 19.7 percent during the same period. All other items remain more or less stable (a 4 percent fall in durable goods and a corresponding increase in financial services are the other most notable changes).[5]

The difference from the revolution produced by the earlier wave of innovations is spectacular. Between 1880

---

[4]Until 1830, speed of travel was determined "by hoof or sail," as Gordon puts it. After that, it increased continuously until the invention of the Boeing 707. It has stagnated ever since.

[5]Clinton McCully, "Trends in Consumer Spending and Personal Saving, 1959–2009," *Survey of Current Business* 91, no. 6 (June 2011): 14–23.

and 1940, the face of the world truly changed. In 1876 Alexander Graham Bell invented the telephone. In 1879 Thomas Edison invented the electric light bulb and Karl Benz the internal combustion engine. In 1895 the Lumière brothers followed with moving pictures and, in 1910, Marconi added the wireless telegraph. The inventions made possible by electricity revolutionized the conditions of human existence: the elevator, household appliances, air conditioning. All these innovations were available by 1929, at least in the urban areas of the United States.

In the brief interval between 1870 and 1900, access to public sewage systems increased tenfold. Between 1890 and 1900 the Chicago L and the New York subway radically changed the urban geography. In the United States, automobiles marked the end of rural isolation and the beginnings of a peri-urban culture. The first television programs were broadcast in 1946. When the improvements made to the innovations introduced in the previous century are taken into account—the railroad, the steam engine, the telegraph and telephone, and the rise in agricultural productivity, thanks to tractors and fertilizers—the full measure of the storm that swept through the European countries and their colonies becomes clear.

Over the last century, these vast transformations have translated into an average rate of income growth per capita of 2 percent annually in the United States. According to Gordon, there is no doubt that growth in the twenty-first century will be (much) weaker, at least for the American middle class. His central conclusion is that the growth level of the last forty years (1972–2014) has become the new norm. The "slow" pace observed since 1973 is in reality a return to the mean, the rate that prevailed, for example, in the period between the last years of the nineteenth century and the 1920s.[6]

Is a new resurgence in growth conceivable? Are we coming to the second half of the chessboard, as the authors of *The Second Machine Age* forecast? Technophiles such as Joel Mokyr like to remind us that scientific progress cannot be predicted. Pasteur would not have been able to develop his theory of microbes without the prior invention of the microscope in 1820. The Web needed Google to become something other than a convenient way to send mail. Paul David's work is another reminder of the fact that the diffusion of disruptive technologies may well take a few decades.[7]

Gordon himself cites the errors of all those who made fools of themselves by announcing the end of innovations in their own sector. In 1876 a memo from Western Union concluded that the telephone had too many disadvantages to be a reliable instrument of communication. In 1927, a year before the release of *The Jazz Singer*, the first feature-length talkie, the head of Warner Brothers asked, "Who the hell wants to hear actors talk?" In 1943 the president of IBM estimated the global market

---

[6]From 1891 to 1972, the hourly productivity of American workers increased by 2.36 percent per year. Its growth has been much lower since 1972, falling to 1.59 percent annually. Moreover, that figure is largely attributable to the abrupt increase that took place with the Internet bubble: between 1996 and 2004, hourly productivity leapt spectacularly, at a rate of 2.54 percent annually, which fostered a belief during that period in a new cycle of growth. Apart from that boom, hourly productivity progressed more slowly, at only about 1.4 percent annually, almost a full point below prior levels. If it is this level of growth that turns out to be the new norm, that would mean, according to Gordon, the disappearance of any prospect for growth for "working-class Americans," once demographics, education, and inequality are factored in. In his opinion, in fact, the gains in productivity in the United States have come primarily from the identification and dismissal of unproductive workers.

[7]Paul David, "The Dynamo and the Computer," *American Economic Review*, Papers and Proceedings, May 1990.

for computers at five. And in 1981 Bill Gates, promoting diskettes, considered 640 kilobytes of memory per unit sufficient. The smallest USB flash drive now has ten thousand times that capacity (we now calculate in gigabytes, which are the equivalent of a million kilobytes). And finally, in 1992, when Bill Clinton gathered together the best minds to discuss the future, no one mentioned the Internet.

Gordon adds, however, that visionaries such as Jules Verne really did foresee the world to come. He even cites an issue of the *Ladies' Home Journal* published in 1900, which anticipated a number of inventions in the making: air conditioning, the automobile, the refrigerator. Trying to predict the future as Jules Verne did, Gordon notes that the items that appear on the list of inventions most often are miniature robots, the 3D printer, Big Data, driverless cars, and innovations in medicine. In the area of health, the twenty-first century promises progress in treating brain diseases (such as Alzheimer's) and controlling transmittable diseases (AIDS, for example). It is not a question of overlooking these innovations but of understanding their potential impact on society as a whole. The techno-optimists predict a revolution to come but understate the one that has already occurred. Gordon believes it would be amazing if innovations continued at the same pace as in the last thirty years.

RECONSIDERING GDP

GDP (Gross Domestic Product), which is used to measure the market value of all the goods and services a country produces in a particular time period, has been criticized as not being the proper instrument to capture the transformations at hand. A number of the benefits of the digital revolution are free of charge and therefore do not appear in the statistics. Growth is therefore potentially underestimated. Angus Deaton, an economist specializing in development, notes that we assess poorly the advantages of owning a smartphone, of having a hundred TV programs at our fingertips, or of being able to access cash machines day and night.[8] When Deaton's parents left their native Scotland to immigrate to Canada or Australia, they had little prospect of ever seeing their families again. The revolution in transportation and communications now makes these separations much less painful.

Gordon's response to this objection is that the GDP has always been undervalued. Automobiles did not appear on the American price index until 1935. Electricity, the elevator, the subway, and the replacement of horses by automobiles were all major innovations that revolutionized urban life but did not figure as such in the GDP, except in relation to installation costs.

One major dimension of the contemporary world is not captured by statistical analysis. Online encyclopedias such as Wikipedia, the data collected by Google, and the pleasure of communicating on Facebook are free of charge; at most, access is granted in exchange for advertisements or the collection of customer information, measures which divert traffic toward the old economy.

There is good news and bad news about this development. The good news is that the Internet offers services that cost nothing, which increases purchasing power. The bad news is that the new economy-leading firms do not generate that many jobs. Even today, Google, Facebook,

---

[8] Angus Deaton, *The Great Escape* (Princeton: Princeton University Press, 2013).

and Twitter combined employ fewer than one hundred thousand employees, half the number of General Motors. The situation is perfectly summed up by a statement from the economist Edward Glaeser: "Highly paid workers work constantly to improve a service that is provided freely to hundreds of millions of poorer users."[9]

Another dimension of the debate concerns public sector jobs, which GDP measures in terms of their cost. The contribution to GDP of a doctor in a public hospital is measured by her salary.[10] The improvements in life expectancy she makes possible will never be taken into account in the calculation of productivity.[11] The same is true for a teacher or a museum guard. Some will argue that real GDP is therefore understated, while others will say the opposite.

The questions raised by the issues around GDP have less to do with statistical measures than with the well-being that is involved with these activities. Following Gordon's line of reasoning, one would agree that the washing machine had a huge impact on the lives of women, while the iPad is just fun. But GDP has little to say on why that is so.

---

[9] Edward Glaeser, "Secular Joblessness," in *Secular Stagnation: Facts, Causes and Cures*, ed. Coen Teulings and Richard Baldwin (Washington, D.C.: Center for Economic and Policy Research, 2014). http://voxeu.org/content/secular-stagnation-facts-causes-and-cures.

[10] Because the GDP measures the production of public employees by their cost, reducing the salaries of teachers and (in France) doctors lowers their (measured) contribution to wealth and also lowers their apparent productivity, which is defined by the wealth produced per work hour.

[11] Richard Landes has noted the spectacular effect of the invention of eyeglasses on European productivity. They allowed many craftsmen whose work depended on good vision to be productive for a much longer time. Paradoxically—given the needs it fulfills—healthcare is now considered a cost that must be cut.

CHAPTER 10

ॐ

Marx in Hollywood

Gordon's pessimism follows in the great tradition of the classical economists, from Malthus to John Stuart Mill to Karl Marx, who announced the coming of a "stationary state," where growth would come to an end. Marx did not accept the Malthusian demographic explanations of poverty, but he did adopt their main conclusions: "Whatever the level of wages," he concludes, "the worker's condition must deteriorate with the accumulation of capital." For Marx, poverty is a social rather than a biological phenomenon. Machines are among the instruments that capitalists have at their disposal to keep wage earners in poverty. The leading classical economist David Ricardo added a chapter to his *Principles of Political Economy and Taxation* (1817), to show the ambiguous effect machines have on the remuneration of the labor force.

Fear of machines dates back a long time. Emperor Diocletian is said to have banned a machine that raised columns because he did not want to "deprive the people of their bread." Much later, in 1811, the Luddites, a group of English textile workers, would smash the new power looms to protest against the threat the machines represented to their livelihood.[1] These are merely two instances

[1] Wassily Leontief compares the role of human beings to that of horses, which, long indispensable, ultimately disappeared as a means of production. The paradox is that horses were never used so much as during the Industrial Revolution of the nineteenth century: in the cities (where horse manure was inescapable), in the countryside, and on the battlefield. Then, all of a sudden, with the advent of the subway, the automobile, and the tractor, horses all but disappeared.

of many. In the second half of the twentieth century, economists sought to appease such fears. Led by the great growth theorist Robert Solow, they argued that machines make workers more productive and thus allow them to benefit from the fruits of growth. Between the years 1945 and 1975, unemployment was at its lowest even as mechanization reached a peak, a circumstance which illustrates the potential benefits of machines: by raising workers' productivity, machines enabled their wages to rise as well.

The arguments of growth theorists rest therefore on the crucial hypothesis that machines "complement" labor. It is said that one good complements another if, like water and tea leaves, they are both necessary for the final product (tea). Conversely, they are substitutable if, like tea and coffee, a choice is made of one over the other. The question today, however, is less whether "machines replace workers" than specifically which tasks they replace, and which survive.

The economist David Autor emphasizes the uncertainty of this situation as follows: according to one survey, 63 percent of economists claim that "automation" is not responsible for unemployment, but 43 percent agree that the new information and communication technologies are responsible for the stagnation of wages in the United States (30 percent are undecided). As Brynjolfsson and McAfee also say, economists hide (from themselves) a "dirty little secret": there is nothing to guarantee that everyone will benefit from technological progress.

THE SAUVY MODEL

The destructive role of machines is often analyzed in terms of unemployment. Machines replace workers, who are then condemned to having nothing to do. Yet it is easy to refute the idea that there are a finite number of jobs available in society, a finite number which the use of machines constantly reduces.[2] In fact, technological progress creates the purchasing power that makes new jobs viable. Alfred Sauvy addresses precisely this question in *La machine et le chômage (Machines and Unemployment)*,[3] calling it a problem of "outflow": work must migrate from the sectors where machines do the labor to those in which they cannot. That migration may be long and difficult, as the transition from the country to the city once was, but it is inevitable. Today we would say that the labor force must move from jobs which can be digitized to those that cannot. But the question then becomes: If the jobs that survive are those spared by technological progress, what becomes of the growth potential for economies? By way of reply, let us look at a simplified model inspired by Sauvy.

Consider an economy that is initially composed of two sectors of equal size. Half the workers, a hundred of them, let us say, are employed in sector A, the other half in sector B. Now let us suppose that a technological revolution destroys all the jobs in sector A. (According to Frey and Osborne, the consequences of digitalization are on that order of magnitude.) The population employed in sector A must migrate to sector B, which, by the end

---

[2] Several examples demonstrate that an unexpected increase in the number of workers is always ultimately reversed. In 1960s France, for example, the arrival of the *pieds noirs* (Europeans who had settled in North Africa, and their descendants) in metropolitan France after the Algerian War did not significantly increase unemployment in the regions where they settled. The relevant variable is in reality the unemployment *rate* (5 percent, 10 percent?), not the *number* of unemployed. I address theories about the end of labor in *Nos temps modernes* (Paris: Flammarion, 2002).

[3] Alfred Sauvy, *La machine et le chômage: Les progrès techniques et l'emploi* (Paris: Bordas/Dunod, 1980).

of the transition, therefore doubles in size. An example of a similarly dramatic change might be the impact of the loss of agricultural jobs in the twentieth century in favor of industry, or later, of the loss of industrial work in favor of service jobs. How are we to analyze the consequences of that "outflow"? What are the properties of that economy in terms of growth and distribution?

To quantify orders of magnitude, let us suppose that, in our example, the migration from A jobs to B jobs takes fifty years, the equivalent of the span between 1980 and 2030. In that interval, the A half of the economy registers infinite growth in its productivity, as the labor once performed by the hundred workers in the sector is now done solely by computers. What is the average growth during this period? Let us assume that, before the technological revolution, every worker in sector A and sector B produced one unit of the GDP. Initially, then, the GDP had a value of 200. Fifty years later, what is its value? Sector A produces the original 100 units without any workers, and sector B, which has doubled in size, now produces 200 units. In all, the GDP has increased from 200 units to 300 fifty years later. It has therefore grown by 150 percent. That is not insignificant, but it means that the annual growth rate is just 0.8 percent, not very far from Gordon's pessimistic scenarios.

How is that possible? Half the economy experiences *infinite* growth in its productivity and, in the end, average growth does not even amount to 1 percent a year. That disappointing result can be attributed to a crucial factor. We have assumed in our example that all the gains in efficiency were in sector A and that the workers in sector B saw no improvement in their productivity. In this example, software quite simply replaces workers, whereas those who are displaced do not become more productive. "The only wealth is man," said Jean Bodin in the sixteenth century. If a worker's individual productivity does not increase, growth is necessarily weak.

FROM DETROIT TO HOLLYWOOD

William Baumol puts forward a model very similar to Sauvy's to explain the crisis in the performing arts in the 1960s.[4] At that time theater actors, dancers, and orchestra musicians faced ruthless competition from much more productive media. A recording of the best maestro can travel the globe for next to nothing, and a movie shown on television reaches millions of households with little impact on their budgets. In this case, sector A in our model is Hollywood. A few stars and studios flood the world with cultural products, which enter homes through broadcast television or cable, almost free of cost. Conversely, ordinary actors, those who appear in live shows, theater, or dance productions, do not benefit from any gains in productivity. A troupe that produces *Richard III*, in recounting "sad stories of the death of kings," incurs the same costs now as in the past. Consumers, given the choice between substitutable products, one cheap and the other expensive, do not hesitate for long.

In this example, it is Hollywood stars who impoverish theater actors. Like software in sector A, they are the embodiment of technologies that allow the production of goods without workers. By contrast, stage actors produce goods without technology. The capitalist, in this case, is the star, the one who profits from technological

---

[4]William Baumol and William Bowen, *Performing Arts: The Economic Dilemma* (Cambridge, Mass.: MIT Press, 1966). Baumol's theory is known as the cost disease.

progress. The proletarian, the actor in competition with the star, must often find a second job as a waiter or a teacher.[5]

This situation is totally different from the transition from agriculture to industry mentioned before. In 1900, 40 percent of the active population in the United States worked in the agricultural sector. The figure is now 2 percent. That transition is a model of successful "outflow." The reason is clear: farmers (sector A in our example) migrated to industrial jobs (sector B), but, unlike in the previous example, sector B was itself experiencing a growth phase in its productivity. The revolution in the first part of the twentieth century thus combined two forces: agricultural mechanization and the surge of industrial productivity.

The transition currently under way is different. For the most part, workers have already migrated from industry to services, and a transition is now taking place in the service jobs that Moravec's paradox leaves to them. The question is: What becomes of the displaced workers? If their productivity stagnates in pizza delivery jobs, for example, the result is unequivocal: the potential for growth will drop considerably.

The Sauvy model also indicates why growth is not only slow but potentially very inegalitarian. If the software producers hold onto all sector A profits, workers' wages stagnate because they are producing the same number of GDP units as before. In this model, even assuming that the software producers in sector A keep only part of the profits—half, let us say—the profits of the super-rich rise to more than 15 percent of GDP, and the growth of

---

[5] Baumol and Bowen note in their book that most live performers must find a second occupation.

the rest of the economy is barely 0.4 percent per year. That is very close to the real figures for the United States.

The United States in reality is two countries. The first has seen levels of Asian-style rapid growth and is populated by the richest 1 percent, whose rate of growth has been nearly 7 percent annually for the last thirty years. The growth of the second country, the remaining 99 percent of the population, is at "European" levels, between 1 percent and 1.5 percent.[6]

[6] Seventy percent of the income growth in the United States between 1993 and 2012 was captured by the top 1 percent. Emmanuel Saez, "Striking It Richer," white paper (University of California, Berkeley), updated January 2015, http:eml.berkeley.edu/~saez/saez-UStopincomes-2013.pdf.

CHAPTER 11

ᐴ

Capital at the Dawn of the Twenty-First Century

The impact of digital technologies leads us to reflect on the key concept of *capital*, which has returned to prominence thanks to the data assembled in Thomas Piketty's heroic study.[1] Two phenomena have combined in recent times: a rise in income inequality, particularly acute in the United States, and a rise in financial assets held in most countries. There is no doubt that these two phenomena are linked. The question is how.

One possible interpretation of the mechanism at work is that the increase in income inequality gives rise to a class of nouveaux riches, whose assets accumulate. Their capital becomes a destructive force for the workers to the extent at least that capital is invested in those new technologies that offer a substitute for labor, giving rise to a new round of inequalities. The problem with this interpretation is that the buildup of assets is in evidence everywhere, even in countries where the rise in inequality has been negligible. For example, the share of total revenue for the richest 1 percent rose from 7 percent to 20 percent in the United States between 1980 and 2010, whereas the increase in France is barely visible, from 7 percent to 8 percent during the same period. Conversely, assets (expressed as a percentage of the GDP) have

---

[1] Thomas Piketty, *Le Capital au XXIe siècle* (Paris: Le Seuil, 2013).

increased from 360 percent to 600 percent in France, while the increase is much more limited in the United States, from 380 percent to 430 percent. How are we to understand this astonishing paradox?

The answer lies in a crucial component of assets: real estate. The economist Étienne Wasmer and his coauthors,[2] analyzing Piketty's data, have shown that it is the rise in housing prices (relative to rents) that explains the explosive growth of assets, not the intrinsic profitability of capital. The value of real property is higher in France, because the real estate bubble did not burst there, as it did in the United States. In both countries, conversely, the capital invested in business has remained a remarkably stable fraction of added value, about 200 percent of the GDP (as in most countries). The value of productive capital has not increased, despite growing digitalization, because the new technologies are typically inexpensive to implement compared to more traditional technologies.

A different explanation is required to understand this rise in financial wealth. To understand its logic, we must take a detour through an additional concept.

SECULAR STAGNATION

In a lecture delivered to the International Monetary Fund in November 2013, Harvard economist Larry Summers, former secretary of the US Treasury, introduced what has become an influential term: "secular stagnation." He

[2] Odran Bonnet, Pierre-Henri Bono, Guillaume Chapelle, and Étienne Wasmer, "Le capital logement contribue-t-il aux inégalités? Retour sur *Le Capital au XXIe siècle* de T. Piketty," Sciences Po, Laboratoire Interdisciplinaire d'Évaluation des Politiques Publiques, Working Paper no. 25 (2014).

borrowed the expression from the title of a lecture given in 1938 by another American economist, Alvin Hansen, after he had just been elected president of the American Economic Association. For Hansen, the slowdown in population growth in the United States was the principal factor responsible for the slowdown in economic growth, which was no longer driven by the need for household goods. Hansen, famous for having imported Keynes's ideas to the United States, concluded that vigorous support for consumer demand was required to avoid a long period of economic stagnation and deflation.

The starting point for Summers's analysis was also the risk of deflation, or rather, the disappearance of inflation. For some reason, inflation abruptly vanished from the radar screens. There are several explanations, but the most direct is the enormous downward pressure exerted on wages in response to the digitalization of the world and the casualization of (routine) work it produces. Inflation is rarely a monetary phenomenon, much more often a wage phenomenon. In response to weak inflation, the monetary authorities must lower interest rates to activate growth. The problem is, interest rates can hardly drop below zero. This is called the Zero Lower Bound problem in the economic literature. It was within that context that Summers announced the return of "secular stagnation," a sign of the current incapacity of monetary policies to boost the economy.

The other problem with low interest rates is that they tend to favor financial bubbles. Take the example of housing. When rates drop, the cost of mortgage loans falls as well. The purchasing power of home buyers increases, at least at first. That inevitably triggers a rise in real estate prices. A drop in interest rates from 10 percent to 1 percent can potentially increase tenfold the price of a property.[3] The same reasoning applies to all financial assets. In the United States, the stock market indexes have in fact grown by a factor of ten since 1980. Only a third of that increase can be explained by a rise in profits, two thirds are the effects of valuations linked to lower interest rates.

It is therefore possible to sum up the link between the rise in assets and income inequality as follows: software puts downward pressure on wages, inflation falls, interest rates as well, and the winners are assets, whether financial or in real estate. It is therefore wage deflation that produces the increase in assets and not the reverse. That also explains why growth in the digital age has been punctuated by bubbles and crashes.[4]

In the end, what appears to be really at stake is not so much whether technological progress is about to stop, but rather whether or not it will lift up the wages and productivity of a majority of workers. The shrinking middle class and the decline in the share of total wages in aggregate GDP point toward the idea that some form of competition between labor and technologies is going on, at least for workers located in the middle of the wage distribution.

[3]Consider an apartment that produces rental income of $1,000 a year. Its value as an asset is very different if the interest rate is 10 percent versus 1 percent. If the interest rate is 10 percent, the value of the apartment is $10,000, since at that price the yield is 10 percent a year. But if the interest rate is 1 percent, the apartment is worth $100,000: it is at that price that the return (the rent still brings in $1,000) drops to the desired level: 1 percent. The increase brought about by lowering the interest rate can be phenomenal (tenfold in this example), and the reduction in interest rates results almost automatically from a drop in wage inflation. Note here that real estate yields collapse. It is not an increase in profit that produces the rise in assets, but its decrease.

[4]Theoretically, bubbles can arise when the interest rate is below the growth rate of the economy. See Jean Tirole, "Asset Bubbles and Overlapping Generations," *Econometrica*, vol. 53, no. 6 (Nov. 1985).

CHAPTER 12

De collapsus novum

While the rich (Western and Japanese) economies have been trapped in "secular stagnation," the developing countries have experienced staggering growth. Since the mid-1990s, the growth rate has been higher than 4 percent annually, a figure close to that recorded in France during the *Trente Glorieuses* era of 1945–1975. Globally speaking, the predictions of endogenous growth theorists, who wagered that growth would double, have come true. We are approaching the third Big Bang of human history: the advent of strong per capita income growth for the most populated countries.

For a long time, population growth in the developing countries was a drag on their development. A few statistics will suggest the scope of the issue. Egypt, an Islamic country, had 13 million residents in 1913. It now has 70 million, and its population should reach 100 million in 2025. Brazil, which is predominantly Catholic, saw its population increase from 50 million in 1950 to 150 million at present. In India, between the beginning and the end of the twentieth century, the number of residents leapt from 300 million to more than a billion.

That seismic shift has been counterbalanced by a silent miracle throughout the world: human fertility rates have suddenly dropped. To take the example of Egypt, in 1950 a woman produced on average 7 children; that number is now 3.4. At the current pace, there is no doubt that the demographic transition (the drop under the threshold of 2.1 children per woman, after which the population begins to decline) will be reached in 2025. The picture is the same in Indonesia, the most populated Muslim country: in 1950, women had an average of 5.5 children; that figure has fallen to 2.6 children, and there too the demographic transition is close at hand. India has undergone the same evolution: fertility rates fell from 6 to 3.3 children per woman during the same period. According to the predictions of the United Nations, the demographic transition will be achieved for the entire planet by 2050 at the latest; at that time, the earth's population will begin what may be an inexorable decline.[1]

How are we to understand the "miracle" represented by this transition? Economists wanted to believe it was a result of improvements in the prospects for growth. When women are offered higher wages, they choose to have fewer children, because they have something better to do than simply embrace their role as reproductive agents. According to Gary Becker, professor of economics and sociology at the University of Chicago, a virtuous circle may then be set in motion.[2] Families have fewer children, and they take better care of the ones they have. Parents make an effort to ensure a better future for their offspring by sending them to school, and the prospects for growth increase. It is a brilliant theory, but it does not fit all the facts. The demographic transition has also occurred in regions where material conditions have

---

[1] Africa appears to be an exception, but in actuality it is not. The fertility rate dropped from 7 to 5 children per woman, and that trend should continue, reaching 2.5 children in 2050, according to United Nation figures. Pakistan is a counterexample that sometimes conceals the transformations under way in the other Muslim countries.

[2] Gary Becker, *A Treatise on the Family* (Cambridge, Mass.: Harvard University Press, 1981).

scarcely improved. It can be seen in the countryside and in the cities, whether or not women work.

The key explanation provided by United Nations demographers is cultural. Women throughout the world have seen on television an idealized life that fascinates them: that of Western or Japanese women whose (on-screen) existence has become an aspiration for female freedom. Brazilian soap operas have proved stronger than the church, which, however, did manage to obstruct family planning.[3] It is a change in mentality, not (just) a change in financial incentives, that explains the demographic transition.

Whereas wealthy countries are facing two internal difficulties—a slowdown in their growth and a rise in inequality—the world in general is moving in the opposite direction: global growth is strong and inequality worldwide is decreasing.[4] From that standpoint, the new wealth of the Third World is very good news. But from one unfortunately key perspective, it is not. This new-found prosperity is not compatible with the conservation of planet earth. If China were to settle into American consumption habits, it would consume two thirds of the global production of grain currently available by 2030. If China's consumption of paper reached the level of the United States, the country would consume 300 million metric tons of it, enough to gobble up all the world's forests. If, following the American example, the Chinese were one day to own three vehicles for every four

[3] See Eliana La Ferrara, Alberto Chong, and Suzanne Duryea, *Soap Operas and Fertility: Evidence from Brazil* (London: Centre for Economic Policy Research, 2008).

[4] Nevertheless, a billion human beings, equal to the global population in 1800, remain trapped in poverty, with a standard of living of a dollar a day. Poverty persists on a massive scale. Only in relative terms has it been reduced. But then, our judgments are (almost) always relative.

residents, the necessary infrastructure in highway networks and parking lots would surpass the surface area currently devoted to rice farming.[5] As Lester Brown concludes, "The western economic model . . . will not work for China's 1.45 billion in 2031." Nor, obviously, will it work in India, whose population will be greater than China's at that time.[6]

GLOBAL WARMING

In 1827 the Frenchman Joseph Fourier demonstrated that the earth's atmosphere traps heat: and if it did not exist, the earth would be much colder. Greenhouse gases (CO_2, steam, methane), in fact, have an astonishing property: they allow solar radiation to enter but trap the resulting heat. As a result, global warming is becoming the most troubling manifestation of the effects of industrialization on the planet.

The concentration of greenhouse gases is measured in parts per million (ppm), the number of CO_2 molecules per million molecules in the air. It has risen from 285 ppm in 1800 to 435 at present. Over the last eight hundred million years, that concentration fluctuated between 200 and 330 ppm, depending on the earth's axial tilt. At the current rate, it could reach 750 ppm by the end of the twenty-first century. At that level, there is one

[5] One of the causes of global food shortages is that crops and fuel now compete for arable lands. It is obviously ridiculous that the fuel industry is government-subsidized.

[6] Lester R. Brown, "Plan B 2.0: Rescuing a Planet under Stress and a Civilization in Trouble," Gaylord Nelson Retrospective Lecture Series, April 20, 2006, p. 10, https://www.nelson.wisc.edu/docs/brown.pdf, excerpted from Lester R. Brown, *Plan B 2.0: Rescuing a Planet under Stress and a Civilization in Trouble* (New York: W. W. Norton, 2006).

chance in two that temperatures will be 5 degrees Celsius higher than the level reached on the eve of the Industrial Revolution. That would be a threshold unprecedented in three million years, the equivalent, in absolute terms, of what occurred at the end of the last ice age. Our civilization came into existence as a result of that temperature increase of 5 degrees; it would be placed in peril were that number to double.[7]

According to scientists, an increase of 2 degrees Celsius vis-à-vis preindustrial levels is the limit that must not be surpassed. Beyond that threshold, disruptions of every sort are possible. Some changes are already apparent: a rise in the level of the oceans, the spread of diseases to regions such as the African high plateaus that were previously protected from them by a temperate climate, increased desertification, and a growing scarcity of available water, combined with the threat of strong acceleration in the melting of glaciers and increased flooding. Other events, though of low probability, would have unpredictable consequences were they to occur. If the Gulf Stream were diverted from its path, for example, Europe would face a new ice age.

A number of complex factors will further increase CO_2 emissions. When the ice in the tundra melts, it is possible that quantities of carbon dioxide will thereby be liberated. The warming of the oceans could also free CO_2 and methane, which are now imprisoned in the waters. Then there is the cryosphere, the ice on the surface of lands and oceans. If the ice sheet of Greenland were to melt, the result would be a five-meter rise in the level of the oceans.

[7]On all these points, see Roger Guesnerie and Nicholas Stern, *Deux économistes face aux enjeux climatiques* (Paris: Le Pommier, 2012).

An average rise of 5 degrees Celsius would mean that certain regions would suffer much more severe increases, of 10 degrees Celsius or more. Southern Europe would resemble the southern Sahara of today. By 2100, under one scenario, temperatures in New York could climb 7 degrees (Celsius)![8]

THE ANTHROPOCENE EPOCH

Paul Crutzen, winner of the Nobel prize in chemistry for 1995, invented the term "Anthropocene" to designate our epoch. It is to be contrasted to the "Holocene," the name for the last ten thousand years. In an article published with three coauthors, Crutzen gives a startling glimpse of the evolution under way.[9] The authors explain, first, that the Anthropocene marks less a change in nature than an acceleration. Human-caused ecological disasters did not begin in the last two centuries, or even with the invention of agriculture. The first *Homo sapiens* to occupy the American continent was responsible for such a far-reaching ecological disaster that mammals (apart from the llama in the Andes) were almost wiped out. The Pleistocene Epoch, which preceded the Holocene, saw the extinction of megafauna, mammoths in northern Eurasia and giant marsupials in Australia. The domestication of animals—which began with dogs 160,000 years ago and came to include

---

[8]Stéphane Lauer, "*Les températures à New York pourraient grimper de sept degrés en un siècle,*" *Le Monde*, February 21, 2015, citing Cynthia Rosenzweig from the Earth Institute of Columbia University.

[9]Will Steffen, Paul J. Crutzen, and John McNeill, "The Anthropocene: Are Humans Overwhelming the Great Forces of Nature?" *Ambio* 36, no. 8 (December 2007): 614–621, https://www.pik-potsdam.de/news/public-events/archiv/alter-net/former-ss/2007/05-09.2007/steffen/literature/ambi-36-08-06_614_621.pdf.

sheep and goats—followed by the invention of agriculture, first through slash-and-burn of the forests, then by irrigation, resulted in vast "natural" upheavals.

Until the Industrial Revolution, however, the impact of humans on the environment remained localized and within the boundaries of ordinary variations. It was with industrialization that a decisive break occurred in geological terms. Before that time, humanity had for the most part relied on renewable energy sources (wind, water, vegetation, animals) for its needs. But the first and second industrial revolutions would have been impossible without coal, then oil (and natural gas). Industrial societies multiplied energy needs four- to fivefold compared to agrarian societies, which had themselves multiplied by a factor of three or four the needs of hunter-gatherer societies. The harnessing of energy resources has allowed a billion human beings to benefit from a standard of living that only kings and some of their courtiers enjoyed in ancient times. Between 1800 and 2010, the population multiplied sevenfold and energy needs fortyfold.[10]

THE RATIONALE FOR COLLECTIVE ACTION

One would like to believe that the age of science has changed the nature of the debate. When, for example, the ozone layer was threatened by the gases used in aerosol spray cans, an agreement to eliminate them was reached. In a different vein, smoking rates ultimately declined in the face

[10] Population growth was itself made possible by one of the key sectors of the Industrial Revolution, the chemical industry. The process invented by the German chemist Fritz Haber allowed the synthesis of ammonia through nitrogen fixation, in a sense turning air into fertilizer. The Haber-Bosch process (Carl Bosch was the manufacturer who assisted Haber) revolutionized agriculture, allowing for the population explosion in the twentieth century.

of proliferating evidence that tobacco was carcinogenic, making it much easier for the government, for instance, to impose smoking bans. Again according to Crutzen, we are entering a third age (the first phase being the change of scale in energy consumption, the second its acceleration), which is the age of awareness. Will it be enough?

Proponents of business as usual claim that global warming is not all that serious, some even pushing cynicism to the point of declaring that there are now enough cities to provide alternatives to the threatened regions, and that it is therefore possible to manage the overall process as it unfolds. The problem with such an attitude is that it raises the formidable risk of irreversibility, taking into account the further increase of world population that is expected. If the climate disturbances were to turn out to be worse than anticipated, it would be impossible to retrace our steps. Crutzen concludes: "By the time humans realize that a business-as-usual approach may not work, the world will be committed to further decades or even centuries of environmental change. Collapse of modern, globalized society under uncontrollable environmental change is one possible outcome."[11]

Is it possible to "decouple" economic growth and environmental damage? It is certainly possible (and the process has already begun) to reduce the carbon footprint of growth. Thus far, however, no one has ever reduced the absolute growth of carbon emissions over the span of a decade. To maintain the objective of limiting the increase in temperature to 2 degrees Celsius (when compared to preindustrial levels), emissions would have to be reduced from the current 50 billion metric tons to 20 billion in 2050—that is, they would have to decrease by a factor

[11] Steffen, Crutzen, and McNeil, "The Anthropocene," p. 619.

of 2.5. If production were to multiply by a factor of 3 between now and 2050 (which would mean an average growth in global GDP of 3 percent annually), the carbon footprint of production would have to be reduced by a factor of 7.5. No technical measures will suffice to achieve that objective. To cite the disenchanted/disillusioned conclusion of Tim Jackson, noted author of *Prosperity without Growth*, "The truth is that there is as yet no credible, socially just, ecologically sustainable scenario of continually growing incomes for a world of nine billion people."[12]

In strict economic theory, there is a simple remedy for excess CO_2 emissions. The United Nations would "merely" have to create a global market for the rights to emit greenhouse gases. Every nation-state would be allocated a quota of rights and could trade them if it so wished at the market price. That formula was adopted in Europe in the wake of the Kyoto conference on climate change; politically, however, such a measure is now completely beyond reach.[13]

Societies are in fact demonstrating an astonishingly weak capacity to project themselves into the future. When immediate costs must be incurred for a poorly assessed long-term objective, the difficulty of collective action is considerable. Human history is punctuated by examples of "broken history," when civilizations had to reverse course. Such was the case for Europe after the fall of Rome and following the first era of industrial capitalism, when the disaster represented by the workers' physical

[12]Tim Jackson, summary of *Prosperity without Growth* (London: Sustainable Development Commission, 2009), http://indigodev.com/ProsperityWithoutGrowth.html.

[13]The carbon tax is an alternative to this system. It has the merit of obliging everyone to pay a given price and of collecting (in a more predictable manner) resources that can finance investments. Obviously, a combination of the two systems is possible.

and moral condition came to be understood. Jared Diamond describes the collapse of other civilizations, beginning with that of Mesopotamia, seat of the first state.[14] The problem, as Mancur Olson has shown, is that the most important changes usually occur after a war or a major crisis. The challenge of the contemporary world is to forge a new framework in peacetime, and, if possible, before the crisis erupts.[15]

In many respects, given the current state of the world, humanity is not yet up to the task of solving global warming. It is unlikely that sufficiently far-reaching collective action can be undertaken solely through the evocation of the risk to the planet. Just as it is too much to require an anxious or depressed person to stop smoking, one cannot expect modern societies, already overwhelmed by enormous worries, to mobilize spontaneously around a planetary objective. Advanced societies, anxious about sluggish growth, have little appetite for measures that could further reduce it, and developing countries do not see why they should deprive themselves of the material civilization from which the wealthy countries have already benefited in abundance. To find the moral and political resources that will allow our societies to rise to the challenge of environmental risk, they must pass through a decisive preliminary stage: they must (re)gain confidence in their ability to build a common future.

[14] Jared Diamond, *Collapse: How Societies Decide to Fail or Succeed* (New York: Viking, 2005).

[15] Enormous research and development programs are needed to produce a sustainable society reliant on renewable energy resources. The storage of solar energy and network infrastructures will require considerable investment, which ought at minimum to be subsidized by some of the taxes and fees on environmental emissions. Daron Acemoglu, Philippe Aghion, Leonardo Bursztyn, and David Hemous present a subtle defense of public incentives to research in that field in "The Environment and Directed Technical Change," *American Economic Review* 102, no. 1 (February 2012): 131–166.

PART III

∾

Rethinking Progress

CHAPTER 13

∾

The (New) Great Transformation

"Since the 1970s we have been going through a 'great transformation' which has destroyed belief in a better future to come. Although a truism, one observation dominating contemporary reflections on the state of society must be pointed out: the social world has changed profoundly." These sober words from the sociologist Robert Castel, reprinted in a book that pays tribute to him, *Changements et pensées du changement* (*Changes and Philosophies of Change*),[1] perfectly sum up the current situation. They mark the loss of an idea so vital to the 1960s, that of a society that embraces the ideal of progress.[2]

In most of the rich countries, this transformation or crisis (if that word still has any meaning when applied to a situation that has lasted forty years) primarily struck the working classes, depriving them of the promise of a better future. "In the 1960s, the working class was triumphant. It embodied and inspired projects for social change. That is no longer the case at all," Castel notes. "The working class has completely lost its drawing power

[1]Robert Castel and Claude Martin, eds., *Changements et pensées du changement* (Paris: La Découverte, 2012).

[2]According to Castel, all 1960s thought was marked by the "contradiction of a society that was forging ahead, that contained enormous resources for progress, and whose merits were officially proclaimed in the terms of a triumph of democracy, and which at the same time engaged in real practices marked by relations of exploitation and domination and by the constant exercise of direct or symbolic violence."

when it comes to social critique. . . . References to the working class are no longer evocations of the possibility of revolutionary change or even social progress. . . . Rather, they point to the scope of unemployment, the growth of job insecurity." Job insecurity is nothing new, of course: it was characteristic of the early days of industrial capitalism.[3] What is new, however, is that it has installed itself in the very heart of the welfare state that was supposed to combat it.

The working classes everywhere have manifested their discontent by breaking away from traditional political parties, on both the left and the right. Bruno Amable does not hesitate to speak in this context of a new "systemic crisis." A comparative study of electoral choices across Europe has shown that the most changeable voters now belong to the least affluent classes, not the middle classes. This situation contradicts political science models, which predict that the median voter right in the center of the political spectrum makes and unmakes majorities. The election of Trump, who gathered 67 percent of the votes of white people without a college education, is a clear-cut manifestation of this diagnosis.

It is an understatement to say that postindustrial society is struggling to find its bearings. Though less visible than the disappearance of rural society, the end of the age of manufacturing has caused a breach that is just as significant. Industrial society was slow to create a reassuring image of itself, through Fordism and mass consumption.

---

[3] Concerns about, and interest in, the condition of the working classes arose in the 1830s. In his famous report, *Tableau de l'état physique et moral des ouvriers employés dans les manufactures de coton, de laine et de soie*, Louis Villermé would describe the fourteen-hour work days of child laborers. http://classiques.uqac.ca/classiques/villerme_louis_rene/tableau_etat_phy sique_moral/tableau_etat_physique.html.

Is it possible now to articulate what a just and happy outcome for the society of the future might be?

THE TWO-STAGE JOURNEY TO MODERNITY

Although the transition from rural society to industrial society turned the economic organization of agrarian societies on its head, the sociological change came much later. Indeed, the social reality of industrial society, in both the family and the factory, retained many of the traits of the ancient world.

The sociologist Ronald Inglehart offers an interpretive grid that sheds light on the novelty of individualism in the contemporary world. He proposes a distinction between two transitions: first, that between rural society and industrial society; and second, the transformation from industrial to postindustrial society. The first break, between the agrarian world and the industrial world, resulted in a transition from a religious to a secular order. People had believed in God, now they believed in Reason. Engineers replaced priests. That first stage, however, still embraced a hierarchical conception of society. The chain of command—from the CEO to the engineer to the foreman to the worker—was as strict as the one from the king to his barons to their peasants. The authorities, previously religious, now became secular. That first transition corresponds to Max Weber's "disenchantment of the world," when magic or faith yielded to reason as society's organizing principle.

For Inglehart, it was only in the second stage that individualistic society arose, concomitant with the end of the industrial world. Under the new regime, self-expression became the founding principle of society. It gave rise to a new type of humanistic society, centered on personal fulfillment. The first wave of "modernization" had led without contradiction to Fascism and Nazism. Hitler was fascinated by Ford and vice versa. That form of modernization had no difficulty molding itself into total-itarianism. It was the second, postindustrial wave that, according to Inglehart, favored the emergence of a soci-ety of self-fulfillment and autonomy.

This transition is analyzed in similar terms in Dan-iel Bell's *Cultural Contradictions of Capitalism* (1976), which puts forward a brilliant analysis of the ambigui-ties of industrial society. The hierarchical system of the world of production is at odds with the consumer society it sets in place. One must be "straight by day, swinger by night," Bell explains. That contradiction is the mark of a hybrid society situated between two worlds.[4]

MAY '68 AND THE RISE OF THE POSTMODERN WORLD

May 1968 was the climactic moment in the metamor-phosis. The attack on the old hierarchical order was launched. Everywhere, in the university, in the factory, in the home, May '68 challenged the established authorities, and it was a phenomenon common to all of the indus-trialized countries. "May '68 was not a Franco-French event," Henri Weber would write. "Its dimensions, its reality, were international from the start. In the United States, in Western Europe, in Japan, it was truly the self-same movement: the same driving forces, the same ideol-ogies, the same watchwords, the same practices."

[4]Henri Weber, *Que reste-t-il de Mai 68?* (Paris: Le Seuil, 1998).

In retrospect, May '68 looks like the high point of an era, just before it began its decline. By the turn of the 1980s, a conservative revolution was already under way, led by Reagan and Thatcher in the United States and the United Kingdom. The speeches delivered against May '68 became increasingly wide-ranging. As Serge Audier has shown,[5] the famous expression "it is forbidden to forbid," came to symbolize the radical individualism of May '68. In the eyes of its denigrators, such as Gilles Lipovetsky, Richard Sennett, or Christopher Lasch, the anti-conformism of May '68 actually ushered in a new conformism, that of consumer society, which requires "permanent novelties" for its continued existence.

According to these authors, the narrowest and most antisocial individualism of the contemporary world would therefore be the fruits of the 1960s. Group conformism gave way to a new conformism associated with the revolution of that time. An analysis of popular songs has shown, for example, a growing use of the terms "I" and "me."

For its supporters, by contrast, the May 1968 movements gave a new life to the philosophy of the Enlightenment, which made autonomy, as opposed to the respect of tradition, a cardinal value. As Tzvetan Todorov points out,[6] however, autonomy as understood by the Enlightenment thinkers does not mean self-sufficiency or individualism. "Our true self is not entirely within us," said Jean-Jacques Rousseau. Enlightenment morality is not subjective but intersubjective. "[It] follows not from a selfish self-love but from respect for humanity." The principles of good and evil are not innate; they must be

---

[5] Serge Audier, *La pensée anti-68* (Paris: La Découverte, 2008).
[6] Tzvetan Todorov, *L'esprit des Lumières* (Paris: Robert Laffont, 2006).

the object of a consensus, which is established through the exchange of rational arguments based on universal human traits.

The emancipation promised by the Enlightenment means that no dogma is considered sacred. The good citizen is one who acts "in accordance with the maxims of his own judgment." It is no longer the authority of the past that must orient the lives of human beings but their vision for the future. For Rousseau, perfectibility is the peculiarly human capacity to become better and improve the world. But he immediately adds that its effects are neither guaranteed nor irreversible. "Good and evil flow from the same source."

The ideas brought by the Enlightment thinkers came into being at a time when the Industrial Revolution had not yet begun. It was the early urban revolution of the eleventh and twelfth centuries that really launched them, by giving rise to a new class of clerks and merchants emancipated from the traditional authorities of church and state.[7] The paradox—and what makes it difficult to interpret modern history—is that industrial society broke the humanist momentum of Renaissance Europe.[8] The secular order would come to replace the religious order, but industry, as embodied in the factories of the nineteenth and most of the twentieth century, were anything but a school for emancipation. For Inglehart, the

[7] During that time period, universities achieved independence by playing on the rivalry between the two powers. According to the historian Jacques Le Goff, for example, "the man of the new era was the humanist, and especially, the first-generation Italian humanist of about 1400—a merchant himself— who transferred the organization of his business to his life." Jacques Le Goff, *Un autre Moyen Âge* (Paris: Gallimard, 1999).

[8] Even among agrarian societies, one would have to single out the "hydraulic empires" such as Egypt and ancient China, which exerted a greater level of coercion than the societies where rain watered the fields. Karl Wittfogel, *Oriental Despotism* (New Haven, Conn.: Yale University Press, 1957).

thread of that broken history would not be picked up until the second historical break, the one that marked the transition to a postindustrial society.

Again according to Inglehart, it was the end of industrial society that gave rise to a new ideal of autonomy. Mass education offered everyone the intellectual means for independent thought. The welfare state broke the bond of material dependence between children and their parents. Communities based on necessity were replaced by "elective affinities." It was in that context that the rise of a postmaterialist spirituality occurred. The search for the meaning of life became the postmodern condition. Materialism declined. In Inglehart's view, everything converged toward a society of autonomy and tolerance: education, urbanization, democratization, and a radical change in the relations of dominance between men and women. Postindustrial society thus liberated itself from the obsession that had marked previous societies, the struggle for economic survival. The tenfold increase in income per capita entirely altered the terms in which human beings thought about their lives.

IS HOMOSEXUALITY A CRIME?

Inglehart does not simply propose general theories. He sets out to verify them meticulously by means of a large-scale sociological investigation, which relies on the World Values Survey (of which he was one of the pioneers) to measure changes in attitudes. On the basis of answers to numerous questions, the survey constructed two axes. The first distinguishes between traditional (religious) values and secular values. The second discriminates between the quest for security and the pursuit of self-expression.

Inglehart's typology, "survival or self-expression," is very similar to that proposed by Louis Dumont and that advanced by the sociologist Shalom Schwartz, which distinguishes between integration and autonomy.

The first axis is built on questions such as: "Do you believe in God? Do you want a large family? Is divorce justified?" These questions allow one to distinguish between religious and secular values. For the second axis, there were questions such as: "Is homosexuality a crime? Is interesting work more important than well-paid work?" The idea was that, in an uncertain, insecure world, people want to be reassured by stable social institutions (family, authority). When the world becomes dependable, when insecurity is less immediate, populations become more tolerant and aspire to greater autonomy and self-expression. Acceptance of homosexuality, for example, is much more pronounced among those who embrace postmaterialist values.[9] Attitudes toward gender equality are another indicator perfectly correlated with the values tied to self-expression.

The countries that place importance on both secular values and those associated with autonomy include Sweden, Norway, and Denmark. At the other extreme, religious and hierarchical countries include Zimbabwe, Morocco, and Jordan. The former Communist countries (China, Bulgaria, Russia) are located very high on the secular scale and very low on the autonomy scale (Russia being even lower than Zimbabwe). On a scale ranging from –2 to +2, France is +1 on the autonomy scale and +0.5 on the secular scale, while Sweden registers 1.5 on each of the two axes. Japan is an interesting case: it is

---

[9]Nevertheless, among the younger generations, whatever their country, there is a tendency to display greater tolerance, and a general shift in that direction is observable.

very high in secular values, above even China and Sweden, but at a moderate level in terms of self-expression, equivalent to France and Italy.

Inglehart, analyzing how the economy shapes society, shows that there is a significant correlation between the expression of secular values and the role of industry (relative to that of agriculture). Service jobs have no explanatory value in this instance. By contrast, the proportion of service jobs to industrial work is a factor for explaining the shift in values from those associated with insecurity to those of self-expression. Autonomy, the main horizon of Western philosophy since the Enlightenment, has ultimately become an economic value. Creativity is valued over authority. A clear pattern emerges from the data. Industrial society leads to the secularization of societies, even while maintaining a fundamentally hierarchical order. It is service jobs that, at a second stage, favor the emergence of a society of "self-expression."

CHAPTER 14

❧

Economics and Culture

The theories of modernization put forward by Inglehart should not be viewed as disregarding the role of culture. Economic data can explain half the variables he analyzes, while the other half lie in the realm of culture. The United States, for example, is a notable exception to the hypothesis of a gradual secularization of society: it displays much more religiosity than other countries with the same economic traits. In fact, when describing the phenomenon, we must distinguish between the English-speaking nations and others with a Protestant majority. In Latin America as well, religiosity is strong. By contrast, societies in the Confucian tradition are much more secular than the others (Confucius' teachings having more to do with social orders than the afterlife).

In the area of self-expression, countries with a Catholic tradition lag behind Protestant countries. They display a lower level of trust, a sign that vertical institutions promoting obedience, such as the church, weaken the horizontal trust entailed in interpersonal relationships. Conversely, the Confucian tradition provides a greater capacity for inspiring trust. In that respect, France and China are mirror images of each other. Of all the rich nations, France has the lowest level of trust (the same level as Russia), and China scores among the highest for trust (at the same level as Finland and above Japan).[1]

[1] The World Value Survey provides a number of statistics on trust.

In a given country, however, the differences in values attributable to religion are negligible. In Germany, for example, Catholics are much closer to their Protestant fellow citizens than to their coreligionists elsewhere in Europe. Likewise, the countries that were formerly part of the Soviet Union are situated at the bottom of the scale for interpersonal trust, even if, like Estonia, Latvia, and Lithuania, they were originally Protestant. That result suggests that it is less the nature of faith that counts than the way it contributes to forging a collective identity. In short, religion is overshadowed by nationalism.

What is really at stake in Inglehart's survey boils down to understanding the ability of modern societies to create social ties among their citizens, especially in the face of the huge economic changes that they need to address. The critical point however, is that cultures can also change in the face of these problems, for better or worse. In order to gain further insights on this question, let us review the three cases of Denmark, the United States, and France.

THE DANISH CASE

The case of Denmark is a fascinating example of a country which, according to international surveys, is one of the happiest in the world.[2] When Danes are asked to rank their sense of well-being on a scale of 1 to 10, the average response is an 8: a grade of A. The other happiest countries in the world are Norway, Finland, the Netherlands, Canada, and, of all places, Costa Rica. The six

[2]The World Happiness Report offers an excellent primer on these data. In the 2017 report, Norway came first and Denmark second.

unhappiest are Togo, Benin, the Central African Republic, Sierra Leone, Burundi, and the Comoros Islands.

Analysts use a wealth of factors to explain the gap between the top and bottom on the happiness scale. Residents in the happiest countries have an income forty times higher than those in the most unhappy. Their life expectancy is twenty-eight years longer. They have twice as many friends to help them out of difficulties, and a higher sense of freedom (94 percent versus 63 percent), and they are less inclined to doubt the honesty of their government (33 percent versus 85 percent).

The global median on the happiness scale (from 1 to 10) is 5; in Europe it is 7, in the United States and Australia/New Zealand 8. Australia, originally populated by convicts from England, has been able to build a peaceful and prosperous society, which should suffice to dispel any notion of (average) genetic influence on well-being. France is in twenty-third place, between Spain and Mexico. It is ranked higher than Italy, Germany, and Japan, which has the lowest grade of all the rich countries, forty-fourth place in the global rankings. It is noteworthy as well that China gets low marks, placing it in the bottom third, between Mozambique and Malawi, despite extraordinary economic growth.

Why does Denmark come in first? Essentially, it is a society where people trust both themselves and their institutions.[3] Three quarters of Danes think that others can be trusted, not only friends or colleagues but, more generally, strangers on the street. It is safe to walk the streets and safe to count on the kindness of others. Journalists from the *Reader's Digest* magazine dropped (supposedly)

---

[3] I follow here the results of the World Happiness Report 2013 and of *The Happy Danes*, Happiness Research Institute (2014).

lost billfolds/wallets containing their owners' address in a number of different locations. In Norway and Denmark, all the billfolds were returned to their owners with the money intact. Elsewhere, the figure was almost always under 50 percent.

Denmark is the least corrupt country in Europe. Democracy in itself is a factor of well-being. Anyone who has seen the TV series *Borgen* will understand the reasons. It depicts the quiet life of a female prime minister, who has to interrupt a cabinet meeting to go pick up her son at school. She knows the game of politics inside and out, knows its share of cunning and deception, but she walks a tightrope, exercising power in a reasonable manner without naiveté and (almost) without cynicism.[4]

Danish society is dynamic. Associations thrive there, and the country has a high rate of volunteerism. On average, 60 percent of Europeans surveyed meet friends, family members, or colleagues outside their work at least once a week. In Denmark, the average is 80 percent. Two million Danes participate in volunteer organizations or soccer clubs or teach literacy classes. The local joke is that, when three Danes meet, they form a club. There are now 100,000 not-for-profit associations. If charity work were assessed by the opportunity cost of the work provided, it would amount to 10 percent of the GDP.

In other countries, unequal access to health, education, and housing causes suffering and anxiety that account for a considerable share of differences in well-being. By contrast, the certainty Danes have that they will be taken care of when sick or helped out if they lose their job is reassuring. That could perhaps be the key to explaining

---

[4]The Danes are not saints, however. Like the other Scandinavian countries and the Netherlands, their tradition of tolerance has not prevented the rise of a xenophobic far right.

the differences between Denmark and the United States, for example.[5]

Work in Denmark is also a source of satisfaction. The country ranks first in Europe for job quality. The Danes are generally happy at work, because trust contributes toward a fair delegation of tasks. The autonomy of workers is higher there than elsewhere. They work 1,522 hours a year, compared to an average of 1,776 hours in the OECD member countries. The autonomy of employees allows them to finish their work at home when necessary: 17 percent do so. Only a small proportion of Danes felt anger (13 percent) or stress (21 percent) at work. Because distances tend to be short, the amount of time spent commuting to work is short as well—and long commutes are one of the causes of unhappiness in a number of other countries. A survey of the sense of well-being among women in Texas placed it at the top of the list of negative factors.

Danish "flexicurity" also protects workers against the risk of unemployment. The policy has three dimensions: a flexible job market, very generous unemployment benefits (lasting up to four years), and an active reinstatement policy. The Danish model is original, even when compared to Sweden, where the level of job protection is higher. The rate of unionization is 88 percent in Denmark, which provides guarantees against the liberties that job flexibility might afford employers. Because the quality of initial training is high in Denmark, professional training is more effective there as well. Everything is done to guarantee a return to employment and to make the transitional period useful to workers by offering proper training.

---

[5] According to a study by Ed Diener et al. cited in the World Happiness Report 2013.

The Danish model clarifies an important issue about the causes of unemployment and its relation to growth. Growth generally favors the creation of jobs. The reason is simple to understand: when growth is strong, hiring is more cost-effective, inasmuch as, on average, firms are assured of finding increased outlets for their products. In a society with a slowdown in growth, conversely, those who lose their jobs tend to remain unemployed for a longer period of time. The lag time can double during an economic crisis, and the jobless rate may also be twice as high.[6] That is obviously hard on the unemployed themselves and on public finances. But if that transitional period is well managed, it can be an opportunity. Given the constant vagaries of employment, it can help revitalize workers rather than demoralizing them. The Danish system has become a model in that area.

THE US CASE

Trust is an essential part of the American psyche, and yet it keeps decreasing. To understand this let us examine the analysis put forward by Robert Putnam in his celebrated book *Bowling Alone*.[7] In 1970, 80 percent of Americans born before 1930 thought that "most people are honest." Only 60 percent of the Baby Boomers (born between 1946 and 1960) thought so. For Generation X

[6] Modern analyses of the employment market consider job turnover rather than the inventory of jobs available. And in fact, the problem is less the number of unemployed at any one time than how long it takes them to find new employment. The so-called DMP model, invented by Peter Diamond, Dale Mortensen, and Chris Pissarides (all three were awarded the Nobel prize in economics in 2010), has become the standard in the field.

[7] Robert Putnam, *Bowling Alone: The Collapse and Revival of American Community*, New York: Simon and Schuster, 2000.

(born after 1960) the figure drops to 50 percent. Putnam puts forward a whole mass of data to document this evolution. The number of people who failed to stop at a stop sign, for example, had increased from 30 to 90 percent! Family life had also become more solitary. At the time of the study only a third of households said that they took their meals together (as opposed to 50 percent twenty years earlier). Seventy-seven percent of Americans interviewed said that their country today had lost its sense of community and that "selfishness" had become a (very) serious problem in the United States. "Rather than turning in to each other, most people drifted apart, becoming more isolated and wanting to be left alone."

No aspect of collective life had been unaffected. Levels of participation in presidential elections had fallen. If one excludes the South, which had de facto excluded Black Americans from the electoral body until the civil rights movement in the 1960s, the extent of the drop is impressive. Electoral participation levels had reached 85 percent in 1960 before plummeting to 50 percent in 2000. Parent Teacher Associations provide another striking example of this kind of disengagement. In 1960, the high point of American civil engagement, one out of two parents was a member of a PTA. In 2000 this number had fallen to fewer than one in five. This collapse in civic feeling is all the more surprising as it occurred at the same time as an increase in educational achievements, and usually civic engagement is stronger in people who are educated. In 1955, 44 percent of Americans said that the time they spent at work was the most enjoyable. In 1999, only 16 percent felt like that. It is not difficult in these circumstances to understand why levels of well-being amongst Americans have continued to fall since the 1960s.

Numerous explanations have been put forward for this transformation of American society. The increase in working women and the number of divorces have been blamed for undermining traditional family values. The expansion of the service sector, by eroding the power of the trade unions, has been held responsible for people no longer taking pride in their work. These arguments are tenuous if not downright wrong. It is simply not true, for example, that an increase in the divorce rate damages levels of civic engagement. With the exception of religion, divorcees are just as involved in social activities as ever, including PTAs, sporting activities, and politics. Nor is it true that the industrial sector has been more affected by de-unionization than any other part of the economy.

In any case, the most important thing about the collapse of civil America is the fact that it happened simultaneously with the rise of the Baby Boomer generation. Indisputably, the generation born after the war behaved differently from their elders. They voted a lot less than their predecessors and read fewer newspapers. While two thirds of young people under the age of 35 regularly read a newspaper in 1965, only one third did in 1990. For the population at large, the level of newspaper reading had dropped by 60 percent even though the average levels of schooling they achieved had increased by 60 percent.[8]

For Putnam, television played a crucial role in shaping the attitudes of Baby Boomers. They were the first generation that was virtually brought up by it. Between 1965 and 1995, the average American family gained an extra

---

[8]As Julia Cagé has shown, the impoverishment of the press (whatever the reasons might be, such as the availability of news on the Internet) explains the rise of the "gutter press," whose costs are a lot lower than those of the more serious press but still manage to attract plenty of readers.

six hours a day of leisure time thanks to a reduction in working hours. These extra hours were entirely taken up by the extra time they spent in front of the television set. Eighty percent of Americans spent every evening in front of the television. Television had "privatized" membership in the public sphere. The American poet T. S. Eliot said of television that it was a medium "which allowed millions of people to listen to the same joke at the same time while remaining on their own." A Canadian study which was able to compare the behavior of two regions that had access to television several years apart (for technical reasons) found that the region which had it first had significantly lower civic participation than the other.

It would of course be ridiculous to impute the rise of individualism which has been observed in the United States solely to television. The cultural shift brought by the Baby Boomers happened everywhere. The May 1968 "cultural revolution," the most visible sign of a generational change in France, manifested itself in much the same way in Paris as the student movement in Berkeley. Whatever the cause, the Baby Boomers began a significant shift in social relations. On the one hand more tolerant, they had also become more individualistic than previous generations.

New forms of community have certainly appeared, with the help of such media as Twitter and Facebook. These are however, using Putnam's terms, "utilitarian" organizations that offer opportunities for "individuals to focus on themselves in the presence of others."

However you look at it, the cultural change in the United States in less than fifty years has been astonishing. The ability de Tocqueville attributed to Americans of forming associations in nearly every possible aspect of life has been lost. Americans still want to go bowling, but nowadays they do it alone without recourse to the clubs and associations which used to unite them. Against the backdrop of constantly declining indicators of well-being, the cultural change over the last half century has not been a happy one.

HOW TO BE FRENCH?

France is another country which fares badly compared to the Danish example. The French are systematically more pessimistic than the peoples of other nations when it comes to trusting the justice system, the political parties, the unions, and so on. When asked, "Is it possible to trust others?" eighty percent of French people say, "One can never be wary enough," according to the World Values Survey. Yann Algan and Pierre Cahuc's *Société de défiance: Comment le modèle social français s'autodétruit (The Society of Distrust: How the French Social Model Is Self-Destructive)*[9] brilliantly opened the debate. In the surveys used by the authors, a strong correlation exists between the level of anxiety of a country's residents and the absence of trust in others. According to Algan and Cahuc, "the psychological cost of being treated unfairly or betrayed in a relationship of trust is at least as important as the monetary cost." In their view, distrust is the key source of the French malaise.

In *Risk Society*, Ulrich Beck perfectly illuminates the fundamental difference between preindustrial risks and those of modern societies. In the past, bad harvests and early death were risks against which nothing could

[9]Yann Algan and Pierre Cahuc, *Société de défiance: Comment le modèle social français s'autodétruit* (Paris: Rue d'Ulm, 2007).

be done. The gods, chance, and destiny were the only forces that could be invoked. Nowadays, we are obsessed with equally catastrophic risks, but we know they are man-made: losing one's job, nuclear war (during the Cold War), or global warming and terrorism. According to Beck, that change in perspective radically alters the meaning we give to the (major) mishaps of life. Losing one's job is not like suffering a bad harvest, even though the consequences are absolutely identical in economic terms.[10]

The French are among the most pessimistic people when it comes to social cooperation. Much more often than in other countries, they think that selfishness governs interpersonal relationships. Two thirds of French people believe that "everyone ought to see to their own affairs without taking too much interest in what others say or do." In terms of trust of others, France is at the very bottom on the international scale, equal to the former Eastern Bloc countries.

French people also have little trust in their institutions. They are wary of market forces and of unions, demanding state intervention, which fosters their distrust of both. But neither do they trust public authority. In France, "the hierarchical centralization of the state's decisions empties the social dialogue" of all content.[11] The Danes, who

---

[10]Freud proposed an idea of the same nature:

> We are threatened with suffering from three directions: from our own body, which is doomed to decay and dissolution and which cannot even do without pain and anxiety as warning signals; from the external world, which may rage against us with overwhelming and merciless forces of destruction; and finally from our relations to other men. The suffering which comes from this last source is perhaps more painful to us than any other. We tend to regard it as a kind of gratuitous addition.

(Freud, *Civilization and Its Discontents*, p. 9.)

[11]Algan and Cahuc conclude their analysis: "To promote mutual trust and public-spiritedness, it is therefore indispensable to break away from the cor-

have greater trust in their institutions, make much better use of them.

Everywhere in the world, a high income in comparison to the rest of the population makes people happier (comparing oneself favorably to others is a source of satisfaction). That is less true in France than elsewhere, however. Individuals in the top-tier professions (executives, senior managers) declare they are less happy than their counterparts in other countries. The low level of reciprocity by employees vis-à-vis their companies is another symptom of malaise at work. According to an analysis by Andrew Clark, only 25 percent of French people agree or strongly agree that they are willing to do additional work to help their company.[12] That is the lowest score for any advanced country.

It is tempting to find an indelible trace of French culture in that pessimism. In the first place, one may (typically) recall that France inherited a strong hierarchical structure, the state, the effect of which was to discourage horizontal interactions. Philippe d'Iribarne's analysis of French psychology concludes that France never managed to reconcile two contradictory cultures: ecclesiastical values on the one hand, aristocratic values on the other. The church champions equality, the aristocracy the opposite. According to Iribarne, the only coping mechanism the French people have had is hypocrisy: they pretend to believe that at church everyone is equal in rank, even while placing people in very distinct slots that fool no one.

---

poratist logic of our welfare state and orient ourselves in the direction of a universalist logic, giving the same advantages to all."

[12] Clark's contribution in *5 Crises: 11 Nouvelle Questions d'Economie Contemporaine*, edited by Philippe Askenazy and Daniel Cohen (Paris: Albin Michel, 2013).

The strength of Algan and Cahuc's work, however, is to show that French pessimism is much more recent than these analyses over the long term suggest (though they obviously remain relevant). The originality of their study is to analyze the evolution of the French mentality in a neutral mirror, the mentality of Americans of European descent, based on the date at which the first generation immigrated.[13] The results of this survey show that Americans whose ancestors were French émigrés who arrived in the United States before 1935 attest to a rate of trust higher than the descendants of Swedes who came to America during the same period. For those who arrived after 1935, the opposite is true. From that time on, the morale of émigrés from France has always been lower than that of their contemporaries from Sweden.

Algan and Cahuc, adopting the theories of Henry Rousso, impute that shattered trust to the "Vichy syndrome," engendered when the French government collaborated with the Third Reich. The French language still retains the trace of that scar: the word "collaboration" is banned from the vocabulary. After the Occupation, Gaullism claimed that France had won the war, which reawakened the culture of denial, a French tendency analyzed by Iribarne. The final blow came with the end of the wars of colonization in Indochina and Algeria, on which France had unconsciously counted to restore confidence in its past greatness. It seems that this became the

[13] Many surveys have shown that the geographical origin of migrants has a significant explanatory power (though this declines over time) with respect to the responses their descendants give to questions about values. The children of immigrants continue to have a level of trust similar to that of children of parents who remained in the native country. Algan and Cahuc's method allows them to neutralize factors resulting from the specific situation of the country at a given time. All the people whose responses they examine live in the United States and are thus subject to the same changing historical circumstances.

beginning of the end of the French believing in their own country. As polls repeatedly show, the French are much more optimistic about the future for themselves than for the country as a whole.

SUMMARY

What we learn from these case studies really amounts to two things. Culture matters if we are to understand the resources upon which modern societies draw in the passage from the old industrial model to the new postmodernity. Second, as the French and the US cases show, cultures do change, over a relatively short time frame. The question that needs to be addressed is always the same: how to bring the citizens of a country together, when the old ties of the agrarian-turned-industrial societies are broken.

The Elusive Quest of Happiness

The notion put forward by Inglehart that postindustrial society has solved the problems of "survival" and thus allowed citizens to focus on self-expression is misleading: it is possible to live in a prosperous society and still fear losing one's job and one's social status, and need to fight for "survival." Inglehart, in announcing the advent of a postmaterialist society, repeats the error in reasoning that led Keynes to predict the coming of a society of plenty, in which people could devote themselves to art and metaphysics.

A fresh starting point from which to address this question of the individual pursuit of happiness is provided by the groundbreaking work of Daniel Kahneman and Amos Tversky, two psychologists who have had a considerable influence on the field of economics. They have shown that human decisions always occur in relation to a point of reference, which changes in response to the surrounding environment. No one is rich or poor in absolute terms, only in relation to their expectations. Whatever the situation in which we find ourselves, in the heat or the cold, in comfort or misfortune, the reality of the world where we make our home ultimately becomes our new reference point. I am happy or unhappy relative to the point I consider normal, which is ultimately the situation in which I find myself. In view of the fact that reported well-being stays the same, despite rising wealth, the pursuit of happiness has been compared to a "hedonic treadmill." Whatever our efforts, we always remain at the same starting point.

Human beings therefore display a formidable capacity for "habituation," to borrow an expression used in psychology. Some authors have argued that Darwinian adaptation may be responsible for that ability.[1] Adaptation requires that one make relative judgments in order to foresee unexpected dangers, and habituation to longstanding situations favors adaptation to one's environment.

Kahneman and Tversky however emphasize one essential point: reactions to good and bad news are highly asymmetrical. In classical economic theory, the pleasure caused by an extra dollar is on the same order as the displeasure caused by the loss of a dollar—one is simply a positive, the other a negative. But that is not how human beings experience things. The pain of losing one dollar is bigger than the pleasure of gaining one. Kahneman and Tversky call this loss aversion.

If one combines these two tendencies, habituation to circumstances and the fear of falling behind, one reaches a distressing conclusion: the fear of going without, the "survival risk" in the words of Inglehart, is just as pronounced as ever. However they seek to avoid it, it always gnaws away at people. If they attempt to get rich to save themselves from want, the position they acquire quickly becomes a new point of reference, and they must begin all over again.

MY NEIGHBORS

What is known as "Easterlin's paradox" translates that tireless and futile quest for happiness into a statistics-based narrative. The economist Richard Easterlin has

[1] Shane Frederick and George Lowenstein, "Hedonic Adaptation," in *Well-Being: The Foundations of Hedonic Psychology*, ed. D. Kahneman, Ed Diener, and N. Schwarz (New York: Russell Sage Foundation, 1999).

shown, based on a large number of surveys, that indexes of satisfaction have been remarkably stable regardless of the level of wealth a country has achieved. The United States may be twice as rich as fifty years ago, but its citizens are no happier. And above all, their financial problems have not decreased. The simplest explanation for that paradox, as Kahneman and Tversky argue, is that wealth is always relative, measured by a point of reference that shifts as one becomes more prosperous.

The other explanation for Easterlin's paradox concerns the obsessive preoccupation human beings have with measuring themselves against others. In 1949 the economist James Duesenberry summarized his studies on consumption with a now-famous expression, "Keeping up with the Joneses."[2] Never fall behind the neighbors in acquiring a car or a television, such is the maxim of the American consumer.

Erzo F. P. Luttmer conducted a study in the United States to measure the effect of neighborhood on well-being.[3] If it is a curse to be poorer than one's peers, nothing is worse than to be outdone by one's friends and relations. Luttmer shows that people are always unhappy living in a county where the average income is higher than their own. According to his estimates, a proportional rise in everyone's income (yours and your neighbors') would have no net effect on average well-being. In France, one

[2] This theory appears in James Duesenberry, *Income, Saving, and the Theory of Consumer Behavior* (Cambridge, Mass.: Harvard University Press, 1952).

[3] Erzo F. P. Luttmer, "Neighbors as Negatives: Relative Earnings and Well-Being," *Quarterly Journal of Economics* 120, no. 3 (August 2005): 963–1002. See also Sarah Flèche, *Essays in Happiness Economics* (Paris: École des Hautes Études en Sciences Sociales, 2014), for an examination and critique of these ideas. A complete overview of the economic theories is provided in Claudia Senik, *L'économie du bonheur* (Paris: Le Seuil, 2014) and Richard Layard, *Happiness, a New Science* (New York: Penguin, 2006).

survey investigated the criteria that led wage earners to think that their wage was "fair."[4] Most of them judged themselves to be well or poorly paid based on comparisons with others; half their reference group was composed of their colleagues, a quarter of their classmates, and the rest of friends or family members. A real-life experiment was also conducted on faculty members at a California university, after the law required that their salaries be posted online. This rule produced frustration and resignations among those who discovered they were less well paid than their colleagues.

The pursuit of happiness in modern industrialized societies runs up against a simple and fundamental obstacle: needs are always relative. What counts is not whether you earn 1,000 or 10,000 euros, but that you know where you stand in relation to the society around you. When millionaires are asked how large their fortune would have to be for them to feel "truly comfortable," they all say the same thing, whatever the level of wealth they have already achieved: twice what they now have.

The crux of the question is the following, however: human beings bow to the law of a desire they do not understand. They are unable to admit that their needs are profoundly malleable. A possible rise in *future* income always inspires daydreams, even though, once it has occurred, the increase is never sufficient. As it happens, people compare their future prospects to their current aspirations, without taking into account the ineluctable evolution of their current hopes.[5] None of us can accept

---

[4] Jerôme Gautié et al., *"Bien ou mal payés?"* Edition Rue d'Ulm, Collection du Cepremap (2014).

[5] See George Lowenstein, Ted O'Donoghue, and Matthew Rabin, "Projection Bias in Predicting Future Utility," *Quarterly Journal of Economics* 118, no. 4 (November 2003): 1209–1248.

the idea that we will be changed by circumstances. The being I am here and now is the only judge on whom I bestow the right to evaluate what is good for me. That explains why growth is more important than wealth for the functioning of our societies: growth gives everyone the hope, short-lived but always revived, of rising above one's psychological and social condition. It is the promise that soothes worries, not its fulfillment.

THE ROLE OF ENVY: RENÉ GIRARD

Economists cannot hope to have the last word on the question of desire. Rather than review the many theories put forward on that topic, I shall explore the ideas of René Girard, whose work on envy sheds light on the issues that are discussed by Easterlin.

Girard's work can be seen as a response to Freud. According to the founder of psychoanalysis, guilt is the crucial cause of the discontent with civilization. This is the essence of the Oedipus complex. Sons love and hate their father at the same time. Once they kill him, they can only love him. Do they feel remorse for having killed the father (in myth at least) or guilt at having (only) desired it? For Freud, it is this feeling of ambivalence itself that constitutes guilt.[6]

René Girard's work starts with a sharp critique of the Oedipus complex. In his view, the sons' relationship to the father has not always been antagonistic, for the simple reason that the father, having long embodied absolute

---

[6]In *Totem and Taboo*, Freud shows that he took seriously the hypothesis of a real murder of the primal father. He returns to the idea in *Moses and Monotheism*, arguing that the Hebrew people did in fact kill Moses in Sinai, unable to tolerate his tyrannical behavior any longer.

authority, occupied too high a place in the children's consciousness to be a source of rivalry. It is the conflict between brothers that makes the world go round. "There is no conflict more common in myths than the fraternal conflict. Cain and Abel, Jacob and Esau, Eteocles and Polynices, Romulus and Remus, Richard the Lionhearted and John Lackland."[7] The source of the conflict between brothers is what Girard calls mimetic rivalry. "For all desires," he explains, "there is not only a subject and an object, there is also a third term, the rival. The subject desires the object not for its intrinsic qualities but because the rival himself desires it. The subject is in fact waiting for the other, the rival, to tell him what must be desired." According to Girard, it is the brother who stands as the rival par excellence.

Girard, in making the conflict between brothers the foundation of violence, reinterprets historically the sources of the Oedipus complex. It is only with the advent of modernity, he claims, that the father's status fell, ultimately approaching that of the brother. "The golden age of the Oedipus complex is situated in a world where the position of the father is weakened but not completely lost, that is, in the Western family over the last few centuries. The father is thus the first model and the first obstacle in a world where the dissolution of differences has begun."

Girard bases his argument about how the conflict with the father functions in modern time on the notion of the double bind put forward by communication theorists.[8] A double bind is a contradictory imperative such as "Be spontaneous!" or "Don't read this sign!" The father,

---

[7] René Girard, *La violence et le sacré* (Paris: Grasset, 1972).

[8] The notion was introduced by Gregory Bateson in 1956 and adopted by Watzlawick et al. in *Pragmatics of Human Communication* (New York: W. W. Norton, 1967).

according to Girard, tells the son: "Do like me, imitate me!" When the son complies, the father reproaches him because he interprets his obedience as an act of aggression, as if the son wanted to take his place. The double-bind structure encapsulates the pathology of a transitional period during which the law of the father has weakened but not collapsed altogether. "The advent of psychoanalysis was historically determined by the coming of the modern world. . . . The less father there is, the more Oedipus does as he likes." Note that Girard implicitly agrees with Norbert Elias, who believes that the West's transition to the age of guilt, in contrast to the ancestral regime of shame, came at a late date.[9]

Girard's analysis allows us to shed light on another surprising feature of the postmodern world: the rise of a new xenophobia, a sentiment that one would have hoped would disappear if a new Enlightment had really come.

In a society driven by the rivalry with others, as Girard sees it, there is a delicate tension between peace and hatred. "There is no culture in which everyone does not feel 'different' from others," Girard explains, "and where he does not think the 'differences' legitimate and necessary. . . . In a society that is not in crisis, the impression of difference results both from the diversity of the real and from a system of exchanges and reciprocity that it necessarily entails."[10]

---

[9]Like Norbert Elias, René Girard analyzes the renunciation of personal revenge as one of the great transformations that occurred during the Renaissance. In his commentary on Shakespeare's *Hamlet*, he analyzes the title character's "pathological" hesitation as a remarkable literary expression of the change in attitude. "Shakespeare turns a typical story of vengeance into a meditation on the difficult situation of a playwright who is sickened by vengeance." René Girard, *Shakespeare, les feux de l'envie* (Paris: Grasset, 1990).

[10]René Girard, *Le bouc émissaire* (Paris: Grasset, 1982).

When society enters a crisis, when the rivalry between its members cannot be peacefully mediated by religion, political order, or economic growth, a scapegoat becomes necessary. "The desire for violence is directed against those close at hand, but it cannot be acted on without leading to all sorts of conflicts. It is therefore necessary to divert the violence toward a sacrificial victim, the only one who can be struck down without danger, because no one will espouse the scapegoat's cause." If desiring the same object culminates in hatred, then shared hatred makes mutual love possible. The scapegoat restores peace. That may explain why, through a strange detour, racism and xenophobia are resurfacing in postindustrial societies, which were believed to be dedicated to tolerance and personal fulfillment.

CHAPTER 16

ॐ

The Double Bind of Work and Autonomy

The moral and political crisis that Western societies now face owes much more to the vagaries of growth than we are generally prepared to admit. Depending on whether growth is strong or weak, individuals are rewarded or punished for their efforts to become respected members of society, whether by finding a job or by measuring themselves against their peers. When growth is dynamic, trust in society is revived; when growth is lower than expected, pessimism takes over once again.

Benjamin Friedman, analyzing what he calls "the moral consequences of economic growth," has examined the major waves of political life in the United States and Europe in relation to the economic climate. The major "progressive" periods of American life have almost always been concomitant with strong growth, whether between 1865 and 1880, 1895 and 1919, or during the civil rights movement of the post–World War II years. Conversely, economic crises sparked the rise of populist movements (1880–1895), the (renewed) ascendancy of the Ku Klux Klan (1920–1929), and the conservative revolution of Reagan during the crisis years of 1973 to 1993.

There are a few rare but important exceptions to that correlation. The most significant were Franklin Roosevelt's New Deal, instituted in the depths of the depression of the 1930s, and the Front Populaire, which was elected even as crisis was overtaking France in 1936. These examples show that politics does play a role. Roosevelt acted to correct Hoover's failures, and the Front Populaire suspended Pierre Laval's austerity measures. Roosevelt imposed his New Deal in the midst of a resurgence of racism and anti-Semitism. Philip Roth's *Plot against America* is a credible (though fictional) account of a victorious presidential campaign by the American aviator and hero Charles Lindbergh, standard-bearer of the far right (to which John F. Kennedy's father also belonged). But the (real) rise of Nazism in Germany dampened the enthusiasm of those in the United States who might have been inspired by that movement.

The tremendous hopes of the *Trente Glorieuses* years in France (1945 to 1975) also illustrate the power of the mechanisms set in motion by growth in the industrial age. For example, when television first appeared in the early 1950s, only 1 percent of the population owned a set. Twenty years later, the ownership rate was the same for managers and for workers. Similarly, the proportion of senior managers who owned a car in 1959 was matched by that of farmers in 1970. On the basis of these comparisons, it became customary to count in numbers of years the wealth gap between farmers or workers and senior managers. Thus it was said that the time lag for the less privileged classes to acquire a car was fifteen years, nine years for a refrigerator, seven years for a washing machine. The miracle of a society where everyone could dream of catching up with the others, even while remaining in place, was thus achieved.

This period is associated with the expression "Fordism." Henry Ford, in the interest of motivating his workers, had the surprising and ingenious idea of doubling wages, in order to combat absenteeism and the tedium of assembly-line work. In his autobiography, he said that he never earned so much money as he did from that moment. His gesture heralded the golden age of an industrial capitalism in which a company could be a site of both production *and* the sharing of wealth.

Following the disintegration of the Fordist model and the slowdown of wages, businesses invented a new system for motivating their workers: management by stress. These new management techniques are perfectly summed up in a report by ANACT, the Agence Nationale pour l'Amelioration des Conditions de Travail (National Agency for the Amelioration of Labor Conditions), cited in Philippe Askenazy's pioneering *Croissance moderne* (*Modern Growth*):[1] "Practices of management through excellence (quality circles, work councils) portray the business as a place of activity fulfilling for the wage earner. The forms of flexibility observed, which value excellence and individual performance and entail frequent rotation for the most demanding jobs, have devastating effects. Frustrations, isolation, seething rivalries, and competition predominate." Burnout is the new malady of the century.[2]

An important share of that suffering can be attributed to another double bind. Wage earners are told: "Be autonomous, take the initiative," even while, through the use of software, the procedures preventing any real autonomy multiply.

Freud said that neurotics were in search of protection against the externalities of the world. According to the sociologist Alain Ehrenberg,[3] the mental illness of our

[1] Philippe Ashkenazy, *La croissance moderne* (Paris: Economica, 2002).

[2] For a recent analysis, see David Blanchflower and Andrew Oswald, *International Happiness* (Cambridge, Mass.: National Bureau of Economic Research, 2011).

[3] Alain Ehrenberg, *La fatigue d'être soi* (Paris: Odile Jacob, 1998).

time is no longer neurosis but depression, which occurs when individuals are anxious about being able to "live up to" the demands of the world. The "economic problem" with depression is that it makes people less productive. Many studies have shown that those suffering from depression have difficulty solving complex problems and even planning their days. Conversely, people in good spirits are better friends, colleagues, neighbors, and citizens. Indeed, happiness encourages cooperation and creativity. If for example, one group of children receives chocolate cookies and another radishes, the first group is much more persistent in solving complex problems. One study estimated the loss of productivity attributable to unhappy people at 10 percent.[4] By contrast, businesses that are listed among the hundred best companies to work for in the United States register a higher rate of return than others, once their specific characteristics are factored in.

Work satisfaction is an essential element of life's pleasures. Sixty percent of those questioned about what they expect from their work cite security, but an interesting job is right behind, in second place (cited by 50 percent), followed by autonomy at work (30 percent). Salary comes in last (20 percent). The effect of unemployment is not only loss of income but also a loss of social status, self-esteem, a connection to other people's lives. Conversely, those who declared as young students that they wanted to succeed financially report lower levels of satisfaction twenty years later, when compared to the others surveyed.

Even in a society at a standstill in terms of global growth, there are ways to motivate wage earners other than through fear. They can be offered careers with ever-increasing

[4] I have borrowed the conclusions of the World Happiness Report 2014.

responsibility, autonomy, and freedom to act.[5] The Danish model is a prime example of a society that manages to solve the problem. Management by stress is counterproductive. The surveys collected in the World Happiness Report show that happy people have an easier time achieving a cooperative equilibrium with their colleagues or correspondents.[6] Those with a sense of well-being also demonstrate greater ease in projecting themselves into the future and analyzing complex information, and they display greater self-control. Curiosity and cognitive flexibility also result from a happy environment.

Work is more than a way to earn a living. In the words of Inglehart, it is also a path toward self-fulfillment. The old hierarchical model, a legacy of ancient times, is coming to an end. It would be sad to waste this historical moment through a lack of (collective) imagination.

---

[5] Legendre, *Ce que l'Occident ne voit pas de l'Occident*.

[6] The prisoner's dilemma, a game that measures people's ability to cooperate, was used to test those in good and bad spirits. The results show that a cooperative equilibrium is achieved with significantly more frequency among people in a good mood.

CHAPTER 17

♋

Social Endogamy

All modern democratic societies are confronted with a fundamental question: On what principles can a society be organized when it remains profoundly inegalitarian, even as its democratic ideals impel it toward equality? This issue, which has become highly critical in the current age of rising inequalities, was already an obsession for Alexis de Tocqueville, who pondered the transition from a hierarchical society to a society of equality. "When all the prerogatives of birth and fortune are destroyed, when all the professions are open to everyone, and when one can reach the summit of any profession on one's own, a vast and easy career seems open to the ambitions of men, and they readily imagine they are destined for great things. But that is an erroneous view, which is corrected every day by experience. . . . They have destroyed the obstructive privileges of a few of their peers, and they encounter the competition of all."[1]

Industrial society solved the contradiction by promising equal access to reproducible goods, even while maintaining a hierarchical organization of production that kept everyone in their place. The postindustrial society had to find other solutions. One of its critical features is that the bulk of what is consumed is social interaction. Where you live, who your kids go to school with, what

---

[1]Alexis de Tocqueville, *De la démocratie en Amérique* (Paris: Librairie de Médicis, 1951), vol. 2.

health services you can get, these are now the reasons that one works. The same quest for wealth remains, but the expensive items are no longer television sets or washing machines but rather a good doctor or teacher to raise your human capital and a good location for housing or vacations. Industrial growth conceived as the infinite production of objects has certainly not disappeared: one need only note the permanent increase in the quantity of garbage and pollution postindustrial society generates. But the time it takes to produce these goods is rapidly diminishing together with their social value. The "old Adam" question: "how to be fed" has been replaced by an even older and more perennial question: how do we live with one another? Despite its hunter-gatherer simplicity, the task is just as daunting. Everyone wants to live with the best and the brightest, and this is not possible.

Gary Becker's theory of assortative mating illustrates wonderfully the logic which is at work. Becker analyzes the search for a mate as a market, the marriage market. In the model that he analyzes, those who were, say, A students in high school end up marrying one another, as do the B students, and so on, down to the D students and high school dropouts. Because the most gifted remain among their own kind, the others in reality have no choice. It is not out of self-love but by default that they turn to the only market left them: people like themselves. The defection of the richest and most gifted has a rebound effect on society as a whole.[2] Almost all individuals, of course, can marry "down" if they do not find an

---

[2]In a study of geographical and social segregation in French society as a whole, Edmond Préteceille confirms that urban segregation is primarily the work of the upper classes. See his "*Registres de l'inégalité, lieu de résidence et ségregation sociale: La société française et ses fractures,*" *Cahiers français* 314 (April–June 2003): 64–70.

appropriate partner at their own level, but they do so only as a secondary resort. Those at the very bottom of the social ladder, who make up the contingents of the left behind, do not have any option but to remain among their own.

Alvin Roth, a specialist in "matching models," notes that the market model is based on the idea that there is one price for one (infinitely) reproducible commodity. But that model, he adds, is the exception rather than the rule, at least for important decisions. Whether for marriage, housing, the schools one's children attend, or work, you make one or two choices, rarely many more than that, and they commit you for your whole life.[3]

As the Becker model illustrates, information and communication technologies can turn into a trap. They claim to improve matchings, create a level playing field: an open, accessible world in which everyone can communicate with others freely, without distinction or discrimination. The outcome may be to reinforce assortative mating. Economists specializing in economic geography have already observed that the reduction of transportation costs did not create a frictionless world. It redefined a new geography that is anything but egalitarian. To take a trivial example, before the elevator was invented, the rich lived on the second floor, the poor on the top floor. Rich and poor ran into one another on the stairs, and even if they did not speak, their children sometimes attended the same schools. Since the elevator has become widespread, buildings are occupied by the rich or by the poor, never by both at the same time. Rich and poor live in different neighborhoods. The city has ceased to be a place where social classes intermingle.

[3] Alvin Roth won the 2012 Nobel prize in economics for his work on what he calls "repugnant" transactions, such as organ (kidney) donation.

Everywhere, a series of closed worlds that no longer communicate with one another is coming into being.[4] Jacques Donzelot has shown how restricted (often known as gated) communities are being established in the United States: the rich build their own ghettos and withdraw into themselves. And Éric Maurin has carefully analyzed the endogamous clustering of social classes in France.[5] He defines rich households as those in the highest 10 percent group (they earn about 3,500 euros a month net). He looks at their presence in the four thousand neighborhoods defined by the Institut National de la Statistique et des Études Economiques (National Institute for Statistics and Economic Studies) to create a grid of France's geography. The results Maurin obtained are stunning: half of all French people have never met a rich person in their neighborhood. That is twice the number to be expected if the distribution were random. The distribution of those who hold advanced degrees is even more inegalitarian.[6]

Only recently, workers, foremen, engineers, and owners were connected by relationships that, though sometimes antagonistic, allowed each group to evaluate where it belonged in a shared industrial world. Now engineers are in consulting firms, maintenance workers are in service companies, and industrial jobs are subcontracted, mechanized, or relocated. Factories are becoming empty

[4]Internet endogamy also takes an intellectual form: in view of the vastness of information, everyone looks for and finds what tends to confirm what they already thought. Psychologists call this "confirmation bias."

[5]Jacques Donzelot, *Faire société: La politique de la ville aux États-Unis et en France* (Paris: Le Seuil, 2003), and Éric Maurin, *Le ghetto français* (Paris: Le Seuil, 2005).

[6]Residential inequality turns into lasting inequality: access to public goods, especially education, is becoming more segregated. Sandra Black, studying the effect of school district on the price of a home in the United States, concludes: "All in all, it is nearly as expensive to move close to the best public elementary schools as it is to send one's child to the best private schools."

places: the jobs are elsewhere, people no longer meet there.

Richard Freeman and his coauthors, analyzing the American labor market, have studied the logic of matchings that occur in the realm of production. According to this study, almost all the inequality observed in the United States can be explained by the inequality in the (average) salary offered by one's workplace.[7] It shows that (only) 15 percent of American inequality is explained by "observable differences" in age, gender, or level of education. Most of the inequality lies in the "hidden share" of differences between workers. Almost all these differences have to do with the company for which they work. Someone employed at WalMart earns less than someone with equal skills working at Cartier's. This should not be possible according to the theory: everyone should be compensated based on merit, it being the responsibility of employers, if need be, to steal away employees whom their rivals have recruited at lower cost. But it does not work that way. A worker's path quickly becomes a destiny, in which the stigma of one's career is irremediable, even in the United States, which believes itself free from prejudice. Freeman's disabused conclusion is that market forces, which are supposed to pay everyone based on merit, turn out to be much less powerful than those produced by the logic of matchings.

If remaining among one's own kind is the way of life in postmodern societies, it should have the merit of relieving the burden of rivalry, of comparisons to others. Society ought to be more peaceful if the "neighborhood

[7]Richard Freeman, Erling Barth, Alex Bryson, and James Davis, "It's Where You Work: Increases in Earnings Dispersion across Establishments and Individuals in the U.S.," National Bureau of Economic Research Working Paper no. 20447 (2014), http://www.nber.org/papers/w20447.

effect" that lies at the heart of the explanations given for Easterlin's paradox diminishes. The United States may have become a very unequal society, but its inhabitants ought not to notice, if they live in neighborhoods where everybody makes the same salary. It is not so simple, however. In a world where, by virtue of the exclusion of other possibilities, only those who resemble one another can be together, resemblance becomes a curse, a prison, producing social claustrophobia for its victims, who keep dreaming of moving onward and upward.

As Tocqueville and Girard explained, a society of "brothers" raises competition and envy. Yet some countries do better than others. Luttmer's findings regarding the negative effects of neighborhood on well-being are not found in Canada, for example. Envy can be pacified, provided that one can maintain the promise of a shared destiny. This is the task of our brave postindustrial world: to fulfill the promise of a new Enlightment, as it was envisaged before the Industrial Revolution, when progress was just about that: manufacturing the right social contract.

Conclusion

Human history has been confronted with seemingly insurmountable challenges and contradictions. When human beings first conquered the planet, impelled by demographic pressures they did not understand, apocalypse seemed "inevitable." As we have seen, November 13, 2026, was supposed to be the day of the last judgment, when population growth would have submerged the continents. The earth as a whole might have resembled civilizations devastated by environmental crises they were unable to control: ancient Mesopotamia, Easter Island, the cultures of the Maya and the Vikings.

Humanity would escape that catastrophe thanks to a radical change that no one had anticipated at the time: the demographic transition, which abruptly reduced the rate of human fertility. A new era began, which the economist Gary Becker interprets as the transition from the reign of quantity to the reign of quality when it comes to having children.

Modern societies, however, remain as hungry for wealth as agrarian societies once were for calories. Like a walker who never reaches the horizon, the modern individual wants to grow ever richer, not understanding that such wealth, once it has been achieved, will become the normal state of affairs, from which she will again want to distance herself. Why do human beings constantly want to escape their condition? It is an impenetrable question, with which psychoanalysts, anthropologists, and economists have sought to come to terms, each in their own words. But the essential can be summed up in a formula: human desire is profoundly malleable, influenced by the social circumstances in which it finds expression. That makes it insatiable, infinite.

Such malleability is both a curse and an opportunity. In reality, it makes little difference where desire finds an outlet, provided it allows human beings to sublimate themselves and to play their part on the social scene. But for these human desires to be compatible with the conservation of the planet, a new transition has become imperative, similar to the one that the demographic transition made possible: the transition from quantity to quality. Attitudes have changed several times in history, but never by decree. They are transformed when individual aspirations and social needs converge toward the same goal. We have reached that moment.

Environmental risk creates a community of common destiny. Those who, like Samuel P. Huntington, embrace a discourse describing the clash of civilizations seem to be unaware that cultures, in the course of their history, have constantly been enriched by borrowing from one another. Benjamin Friedman, analyzing international surveys on well-being, makes a key observation. In the 1960s, Cuba, the United States, and Nigeria expressed the same quantum of happiness, regardless of their relative level of income. International surveys on well-being currently show that countries rank themselves in relation to one another in the same way as individuals within a single country: the richest are happiest because they are highest on the scale of comparisons. The most plausible explanation, according to Friedman, is that people in the past compared themselves to their close neighbors, whereas they now find models on television or in the distant communities to which they are connected through the Internet. That is bad news, inasmuch as the need for imitation raises the risk that CO_2 emissions will soar. But it also proves that human beings now have the ability to think of their social relationships in global terms.

To mobilize the peoples of different nations, however, it will not suffice to count solely on the threat of environmental disaster. In his book *La voie* (*The Path*),[1] the French sociologist Edgar Morin sums up the stakes of what he terms a "politics of civilization": "A society cannot make progress in complexity, that is, in freedom, autonomy, and community, unless it also makes progress in solidarity. A politics of civilization must aim toward restoring solidarities, rehumanizing cities, revitalizing the countryside."

We must invest in a new urban civilization that avoids ghettos and, as much as possible, mitigates social endogamy. Architects tell us that a compact city can be green if it is provided with the resources.[2] Tests have been done to evaluate the emotions of students going from their dormitories to their classrooms, either by taking a long, roundabout path through the woods or a simpler and faster tunnel underneath the university. Obviously, higher satisfaction comes from taking the path through the forest, even though it is longer, but the differential astonished even those conducting the experiment. Other tests point in the same direction. Hospitals whose rooms have a garden view record a higher rate of cure than others. The need for nature is still very much here, in the core of our civilized world.

Western civilization, following Morin, can take pride in the best parts of itself: critical thought, democratic principles, the rights of men, women, and children. Traditional societies maintain a sense of being included

---

[1] Edgar Morin, *La voie* (Paris: Fayard, 2011).
[2] Olivier Mongin, *La ville des flux* (Paris: Fayard, 2013).

within nature and social bonds of community, virtues which they must conserve even while incorporating into themselves the best of the West, and which the West must reinvent for itself.

To follow Morin's conclusion: "A regeneration of political thought must be grounded in a threefold conception of humanity: as individual, as society, and as species." In that program, every phase is necessary to every other: the individual cannot think of herself as representative of a species to be protected, unless she has previously found a sense of shared community in the society where she lives, works, and desires. This makes a good program for the twenty-first century, as good for us as it was for the first herd of hunter-gatherers who decided to cross the sea.

Index